The
Magic
of the
State

How foolish it would be to suppose that one only needs to point out this origin and this misty shroud of delusion in order to destroy the world that counts for real, so-called "reality." We can destroy only as creators.

Nietzsche, The Gay Science

The Magic of the State

Michael Taussig

Routledge
New York and London

Published in 1997 by
Routledge
29 West 35th Street
New York, NY 10001

Published in Great Britain by
Routledge
11 New Fetter Lane
London EC4P 4EE

Copyright © 1997 by Routledge

Printed in the United States of America on acid-free paper.

Library of Congress Cataloging-in-Publication Data

Taussig, Michael T.
The Magic of the state / Michael Taussig.
p.   cm.
Includes bibliographical references.
ISBN 0-415-91790-5 — ISBN 0-415-91791-3
1. Political culture—South America. 2. Allegiance—South America.
3. Patriotism—South America. 4.Martyrs—South America. 5. Spirit
possession—South America. 6. Symbolism in politics—South America.
7. South America—Colonial influence. I. Title.
JL1866.T38   1996
320.98—dc20
                                                    96-13469
                                                        CIP

□ —— ACKNOWLEDGMENTS

I would like to thank the students in the Department of Performance Studies of New York University who took *The Magic of the State* seminar in the fall of 1987 and with whom I initiated the basic ideas herein.

Three artists, Ofelia Moscoso, Susana Amundaraín, and Sara Maneiro, were enormously kind and enormously helpful in my gaining insight into the imagery and spirit possession at issue here, yet in no way can they be held responsible for my varied flights of fancy.

Rarely could an author have had such patient, calm, and imaginative editors as Bill Germano and Matthew DeBord of Routledge.

Rachel Moore suffered a grievous blow to the face during research for this work, but her smile remains as radiant as her mind, its effervescent and at times wickedly humorous light floating on every page that follows.

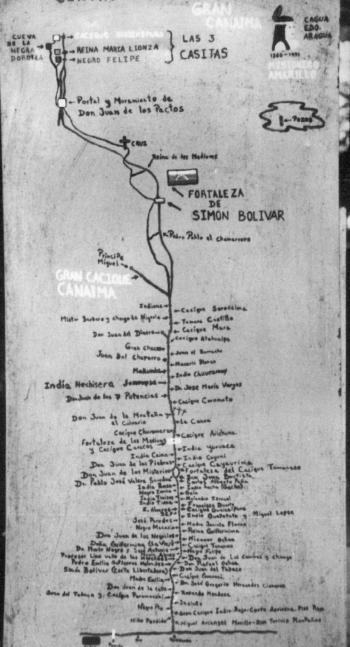

CONTENTS

A Note
on Names
and Naming

Torn between the overlapping claims of fiction and those of documentary, I have allowed this magic of the state to settle in its awkwardness in the division of the forms. I have changed the names of places and people where necessary to preserve anonymity, but also to render more adequately the fictional features without which documentary, including history and ethnography, could not be. Through something like Brecht's estrangement-effect, naming as renaming can provide insight into what we call history, its making no less than its retelling, especially history of the spirits of the dead as the mark of nation and state, but I have in mind, by renaming, some-thing else as well — namely the evocation of a fictive nation-state in place of real ones so as to better grasp the elusive nature of stately being. After all it is not only the writer of fiction who fuses reality with dreamlike states. This privilege also belongs, as Kafka taught, to the being-in-the-world of the modern state itself.

PART ONE

THE SPIRIT QUEEN'S COURT

MARIA LIONZA – REINA DE LA MONTAÑA

I — *The Spirit Queen*

How naturally we entify and give life to such. Take the case of God, the economy, and the state, abstract entities we credit with Being, species of things awesome with life-force of their own, transcendent over mere mortals. Clearly they are fetishes, invented wholes of materialized artifice into whose woeful insufficiency of being we have placed soulstuff. Hence the big S of the State. Hence its magic of attraction and repulsion, tied to the Nation, to more than a whiff of a certain sexuality reminiscent of the Law of the Father and, lest we forget, to the specter of death, human death in that soul-stirring insufficiency of Being. It is with this, then, with the magical harnessing of the dead for stately purpose, that I wish, on an admittedly unsure and naive footing, to begin.

What it is about the dead that makes them so powerful in this regard, I do not know. Could it be that with disembodiment, presence expands? Language is like that too. In fact language depends on this lingering on as an idea tracing an outline around a once solid, breathing form, troubling the body's once bodiedness. Circling endlessly, now and again pausing for breath, words and things, drifting apart, coming together. If only for the moment, death stills the circuit in a frenzy of anxious embodiment-lust — just as spirit possession and shock can do, types of death holding spirit and body at arm's length from one another. Eyeing each other. Imagine the tension. The shoot out at the OK Corral. Your metaphor. My literality. Just the quiet, occasionally interrupted by the stamping of hooves. In the stillness of this stand-off where death interrupts the circle of exchange between the real and the figure of the real, time turns on itself and there begins the glow, the glow of the strange after-life akin to an after-image that surges from radical incompleteness, which is, perhaps, an odd way of putting it — this constant surging, the incompleteness of life, staggering along, now this way, now that, then physically ended and given some sort of narrative structure by posterity, another form of incompleteness, really, too definitive a bodily closure on what might have been. Which is why the soul is so important, the indispensable relic that holds open the possibilities for the might have been — back then, and over there.

And because I feel that I am more known by this than knowing, as though there were an ultimate yet elusive truth in death, inaccessible to people like me for whom death has been supremely sterilized, not to mention repressed and further mystified, I hope to clarify matters somewhat, and not only for myself, by thinking about the magic of the state in a European Elsewhere — your metaphor, my literality — as related by a free spirit who frequented those parts, a sunny place, she said, from where oil flows out, cars, ammo, and videos flow in, and where a crucial quality of being is granted the state of the whole by virtue of death, casting an aura of magic over the mountain at its center.

Imagine, she had said, imagine the live bodies trembling there on the spirit queen's mountain rising into the mist sheer from the plain where ghostly laborers tend the sugar cane and clouds swirl around high-voltage pylons. Imagine what it means to enter that space where she rules over the courts of spirits swarming there together with the serpents and the dragons. Imagine your body in its spasmodic resurrection of those who died in the anti-colonial wars that founded the state of the whole. That, my friend, is really something!

She smiled.

Yes! A whole type-cast set of spirits of Europe's Others; the fierce Indians who fought the early *conquistadores*, the African slaves and freedmen, and then all manner of riff-raff insinuated into the hearts of the people the past few years; Vikings like Eric the Red, not to mention fat smiling Buddhas and cruel dictators who sunk this country in blood turning neighbour against neighbour; all in all an impossible mix, a fantastic martyrology of colonial history enlivened and derailed by inexplicable meanderings. . . . And her voice trailed off as if she, too, in her effort to explain, had succumbed to the impossibility of that very imagining and was about to be silenced forever as glowing image in that luminous space of death recruited with such perfection by the fantasy theater of the state of the whole.

She held out her hands in mock despair as if searching for an image adequate to convey the character of death enlarging life under the banner of the state thrust brazenly at the elements. It was the extremity of it all, the extremity of the figures, the extremity of the changes, the passion no less than the stupefaction. Where a mere flick of a gesture towards the literal was intended by stately poetics, here, in the theater of spirit possession, death-work excavates the wordless experience within submission no less than within the power to command.

She leaned forward as if challenging me. And doesn't a caricature capture the essence, making the copy magically powerful over the original? And what could be more powerful than the modern state? For the world of magic is changing, has changed. . . . Wasn't it Lenin himself who wrote in 1919 that now nearly all political disputes and differences of opinion turn on the concept of the state, and added "more particularly on the question: *what is the state?*" — and her voice trailed away with the wonder of it all, that the primary political thing could be so taken for granted yet be so utterly opaque and mysterious that at the end of all her pontificating she was driven to an awkward silence, aware that sooner or later there was this perfidious contagion of power, that might made right no less than right made might. Was this the magic she was referring to, and in that case would self-awareness help any, or was something else required?

She grabbed my wrist. You want to know the secret, don't you?

Slowly she released her grip and when she spoke her voice held the forlorn note of someone unsure as to whether she would ever be understood, poised, as she was, on the brink of stupendous truths that any moment could collapse under their own weight. The labor of the negative, she sighed, and the whole mad scheme unplanned as if it were there all along with the invention of the state, the form within the form with its danger and with its decay too, underbelly of stately prowess and sanitized rigidity. Only people with a superb talent for the theater could pull this off. And you too can be part of this. After all, it touches every one of us. If you miss your chance now, you miss it forever!

And this death-space?

Not life after death, she replied, but more edge to life, now they're pure, pure image, these spirits stalking there where together Europe and its colonies, white and colored, reflect back stunning fantasies of each other's underworlds from conquest and slavery onward, brimful with the vivacity of treachery and obscure design. A strange beauty, despite the magnificence of evil and the idiosyncrasies of its inhabitants, wellspring of the imagination where the Last Judgment on History never ceases, so many stories erased, so many repressed, the simplifications, the passions—blessed are the *caudillos* raging wild through time and space—the passion of armed combat, the anti-colonial wars, the even greater wars within those wars of class against class, colored and white, the bullshit piled higher and higher, a storm of bullshit awaiting the golden buckets of the Redeemer. More a contorted presence than a space, an eye-bulging dangerous presence at that, so full it is of half-rendered beings and amputees of history looking for a substantial body with which to act and re-enact, bursting the dams of memory.

But what sort of body could contain that history, let alone give it adequate shape? Is this the body of woman that is the mountain rearing high above the plain, clouds tumbling? Is this the body of woman, more presence than image, shrines as gateways bedecking her capacious being like jewels, glowing entry points into the jumble of lives cut short that here in this charged space erupt into the possessed body as foaming silhouettes etched from the cliches of the founding violence—as remembered—the colony shaken free of old Europe in a massive bloodletting of class warfare and populist rage no less directed against the white creole patrician class than led by the latter against the colonial power? The great killers with the supernatural grace that killing endows—"he ate with them, he slept among them, and they were his whole diversion and entertainment" (Boves and his black cowboys). "War to the Death." The famous proclamation of January 16th, 1813, taken up by the Liberator. "Do not fear the sword that comes to avenge you and to sever the ties with which your executioners have bound you to their fate." Oh yes my friend! You will hear more of this sword despite its size, this sword that severs fate, she said, twirling her golden flag on which was embroidered "Goddess of the Harvests and the Waters."

She smiled and took up where she'd left off. The edge of the cliffs lit up for an instant where long long ago the sea had been, leaving those stark rock faces. And still I can see her there become so much stronger than he ever was alive. You don't see flags like that anymore, carnivalesque and once upon a time fancy free like up north with symbols such as pine trees, beavers, anchors, and rattle snakes, bearing slogans such as "Liberty or Death," "Hope," "An Appeal to Heaven," "Don't Tread On Me," or down south with an Indian holding aloft the symbols of the French revolution while seated on an alligator bearing the message of freedom from old Europe. Even today with flags so severe, standing for nations as they do, with two or three stripes of primary color and stars in rows regimenting the very heavens, even so, kids love them and as she talked I wondered whether it could be that death and the children meet on this very point to constitute the magic of the state?

But here I was, once again, descending into obscurity as irony crept into her world-weary voice. The European Elsewhere has here perfected the European ideal, she said. Wasn't it Hegel, that most Eurocentric of philosophers who thought the modern state was born in the terror of revolution so as to realize the Christian synthesis not after death but on earth during life? Exactly! That's what goes on here. Thanks to spirit-possession, death is fast-forwarded into life. Quite an advance, really. Not that it's easy or ever guaranteed. Indeed, that's the point. She paused, searching her memory. "The life of the mind endures death and in death maintains its being. It only wins to truth when it finds itself utterly torn asunder. It is this mighty power only by looking the negative in the face and dwelling within it."

Beholden, we are, to those who go to the mountain to make their shrines to become possessed by the dead wandering footloose and fancy free from their abode in the National Pantheon. And what a pantheon! Pell-mell they pour out, evacuees from the state's marbled interior, frightened and delirious with their new-found freedom, too much freedom, the low-lifes scouring the land for a puddle, a dark drain, or a warm, live body, the nobility like the wild Indians and Africans uniting finally in the body of woman that is the mountain rising sheer from the cities of the plain. Hustling into present-time. Woman's time. Her eyes blazed. She was like someone possessed. The mountain. The way it holds the state of the whole! Like a fable. Like a stage, but real, on which the dead who are said to have made the whole are brought back to inhabit the bodies of the living, lying still under the trees concentrating the quietness into themselves, others kicking and screaming, walking on fire, skewering themselves with needles from which hang the national colors.

Oh! No! She went on, looking up. It's not the weirdness of the pilgrims. To the contrary. It's the weirdness of the state.

Here is a picture of the European Elsewhere. She was more a recorder, as you can see, than an artist.

Is this a real place? I asked?

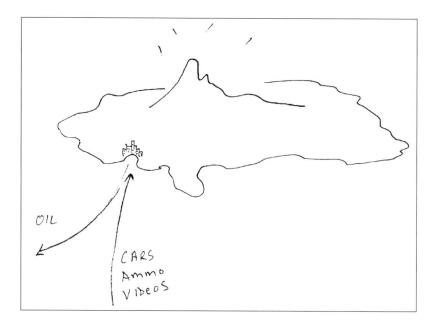

No more, no less, than any other. She smiled. Only the names have been changed to protect the innocent.

It's more a question of what it is that seems to make a place real, she continued, making a wavy motion with her hands, where the shapely solidity of space, gives way to its meaning. . . . Her hands hovered like bats' wings over her sketch. Shapely solidity indeed.

Places are real enough, in their way, she went on, gesturing at the picture, her eyes narrowing to points of flame as darkness descended and crescent moons flashed, but after all what's at stake here is a crucial quality of being granted the state of the whole. That's not so much real as surreal — and that, she hissed, is a question of fear and seduction. She was an impossible being, holding dissimilar things together, bringing the back-then and the over-there slap up against the here-and-now, hovering between estrangement and familiarization.

Then I ask myself, she said, what do you want when you want knowledge? Nothing more than this. Fear drives you to reduce something strange to something familiar so you no longer marvel at it. And then the familiar itself becomes more difficult to see as strange. Is that what the trick takes, I wondered, to abut the here-and-now with the back-then and over-there so you see your world anew?

And then, and only then, characters emerge who make time stop and dreams erupt in the face of great peril into which I too must enter.

But do the resources exist for this estrangement? The figures? The moods?

She looked away. I felt sorry I'd pushed her into a search for a method. I was being unfaithful. Our pact had always been to steer clear of that. Method was like a drug.

It's the danger, she said. The underground caverns. The disappearances. The going mad. The killers and the rapists. And the beauty . . . the waterfalls, the soaring green of the mountain, the shrines so pretty, blinking with the fury of their images and candles, the bodies laid out one after the other. Who would take that risk? Letting that tumultuous crew tumble into our time. Dread shot through with uplift. She was jabbing her finger, the one with the ring with the red rose, at the picture of the mountain. Her voice had a tired and angry edge. And the emptiness. Gaudiness. Decay. Glassy-eyed superstition. The usual suspects. Altars slowly washed away. Outlines of the human form in talcum powder passing into the mud. Garbage. Ugly slabs of concrete crumbling under the marching feet of centipedes. Vacant stares. Congealed visions run rancid.

What words to use? she went on. Old words, leaden words, pompous and heavy on the tongue, primal words with double meanings. Sacred/Accursed. Holy/Polluted. Power born in transgression. Overused words that through priestly control mean nothing any more. The tragedy it all began with. The original sacrifice, endlessly repeated. Or was it a crime? With whom do we identify? The victim or the killer? They took the power, cruel and beautiful and hard to pin down as it was. But why do I feel compelled to put it in a story? Before and after. Our fate to be always after. So we strive for another way of saying these things. Does transgression merely suspend the taboo? "Lightning and thunder require time," he had said. "The light of the stars requires time. Deeds, though done, still require time to be seen and heard." And beyond the body the death-space. To feel its power. To spend that power. To scatter it to the four winds. I ask you in all honesty, I ask myself, would justice be possible without this?

We remember the Indians. Always after. Now they flood back in glory, *caciques*, warriors, gathering force here in the spirit queen's mountain rising sheer from the plain with the clouds tumbling through the high voltage pylons. Hegel remarks that all facts and personages of importance occur in world history, as it were, twice. But he forgot to point out that the first time is as tragedy, the second as farce. In the making of modern nations, the dead do double duty. Out of nowhere, it seems, people conjure up a slice of deadness and borrow from it their names, battle cries, and costumes, in order to present the new scene of world history in dazzling form until reaction sets in and the spirit of revolution gives way to ghosts retracing their steps . . . we remember the Indians. . . . Yes! They do double duty and the tradition of the dead generations weighs like a nightmare on the brain of the living. Not even the dead shall be safe, and the angel of history, eyes staring, mouth open, trying to waken them, is a born loser, wings crumpled in the storm blowing from paradise. Raging back and forth, island hopping from swamp to high mountain, take no prisoners, just corpses, freedom promised the slaves to stop them fighting for the crown, nowhere did so many deaths occur as on the mountain of dead now rising sheer from time, tiered in courts — death from war and pestilence, diarrhea exsanguinating the mercenaries in their scarlet uniforms dissolute and lost after years of service in the Napoleonic Wars to find themselves back home in Ireland and England jobless and drawn to fight for freedom in the tropics. Pitiful. (And O'Leary, your statue never even made the National Pantheon!) Nowhere did so many die as died on this soil to liberate a continent. And then the death-in-life of the dictatorships, one after the other. Nowhere in the entire continent were there so many for so long as from here. (Not that it was a competition.)

And then the Church! Nowhere in the continent was the loss of influence felt so early. Nowhere was it so complete. The death-blow came in the late nineteenth century with "The Illustrious American, The Pacificator and Regenerator, Dissipator of Anarchy." He reduced the Church to an object of contempt, it is said in a learned tome published in 1933, such that it became "incapable of consolidating the loyalty and devotion of the people" — and his anti-clerical legislation still stands today.

□ — *"The Illustrious American: The Pacificator and Regenerator, Dissipator of Anarchy."*

Like the *conquistadores* erecting churches over the ruins of Indian temples, the Dissipator of Anarchy broke down the walls of the Convent of Immaculate Conception in the center of the capital and forcibly expelled the nuns so as to build his new government buildings, the Federal Palace and the Capitol — nicely adorned with the paintings of the nationalist school, painted in Paris, depicting the heroic exploits of the great anti-colonial wars (but not of the wars within those wars). In the plaza just opposite the convent stood the new bronze statue brought from Europe, of the Liberator on his prancing steed. At its unveiling, electric light was used for the first time in the state of the whole. As a young man the Dissipator of Anarchy had invented the slogan, "Federalism, Immaculate and Sacred." The Church was not so much destroyed as recast as political theology on its original footing of violence, sacrifice, and spectacle. But, you know, she said after a few moments, pursing her ruby lips, the problem with that is it's so easy to screw up. First time tragedy, second time. . . . No! It's beyond farce. It turns on itself as parody and, mixed with terror, bleeds into the mute-absurd for which kitsch is the satisfying resolution.

You know, she went on, the park the Dissipator of Anarchy built to himself at Calvary reminds me in some ways of the spirit queen's mountain. It used to be a cemetery. He removed the cadavers and skeletons and built beautiful gardens with perfumed trees through which led a winding road to the summit. It was called the Promenande of the Illustrious American and served, said an eyewitness, as the principal lung of the capital. On holiday nights his statue was illuminated there by little oil lamps which were strung on wires about the pedestal, appearing to the peons of the plantations and charcoal burners in the mountains, said the eyewitness, to be rising from a cauldron of fire. But who knows what the peons were thinking? she asked. Yet the person who described this got something right; the banality, the high camp, the state as work of art, so many variations

on Calvary. Perfumed and all. . . . So there you have it, she said abruptly. A sunny place, where oil comes out, cars, ammo, and videos, come in, and men pass into history as postage stamp replicas of the Liberator. Stamps; the visiting cards of nations left in the bedrooms of children. Aspects of the official.

And they say — but you know how much they say — that the police, the army, and even the President are among the foremost worshippers of the spirit of the mountain, the spirit-queen, that is, the one who runs the whole show, left-hand, woman, woman's time. What time is that? Eternity? The gift of faith. Promises granted. But the price? Is there a price? Must there be a price? Some say so. And are scared. Others see an embarrassment of riches. A mountain of excess. The guardians prowling below. The decay. The gloom descending. The rain dripping from the haze on the mountain where life and death ferment in the dankness of plastic everywhere, holy and unclean, garbage everywhere, rocks painted with the national colors, caves with their interiors painted with the national colors, people lying still in front of their shrines under giant trees in the stillness of the night. Still! Its beyond stillness. Like the interval waiting after the last heartbeat. And beautiful like you'd never believe.

I never cross the river without my knife.
It's different for men, I guess.
Impossible to describe, really.

He came bounding out of nowhere. It was a weekday. Nobody there. Just the buzzing of insects. Butterflies looping through sunbeams. Iridescent. She was beating the drum, slowly. Boom! Boom! Seemed an effort. Wasn't a drum, really, but an old tin can she'd found behind the shrine. Haydée was stretched out on the ground, pale as a ghost. Her red hair. Surrounded by burning candles, the flames vibrating like the insects. Boom! Boom! All the time the Indian looking down on us. Serene. And below the Indian the Liberator and the half head of the spirit queen herself by the side of the Liberator and that print of the sacred hand of Jesus. He came bounding out of nowhere, long-legged with his magic wand. Or was it a sword? He went straight up to Haydée — if you could still call her Haydée, I mean, without her spirit and all — touched her with the wand looking down on her in her trance, pale, unconscious, and proclaimed in the name of the spirit queen and the African Court, and the Medical Doctors' Court, and it went on and on, then leapt away. Years later a friend of mine was raped by one of the guardians at that spot.

Bodies open. Different for a man, I guess. You'll never understand what holds the whole together until you can face that!

Let me tell you about it, she said, handing me a *tabaco*. We lit up. My head swam. Her voice was different. No justice without force, she said. Her sloganizing was exasperating. She grabbed my wrist. And get this my friend. This is not a violence external to law or to reason. Through the smoke I could see her staring at the ash. I heard waves of sound cascading across the canefields, coming closer, the world opening to an infinitude of frogs chanting at the rising moon, their backsides vibrating, the millennial mud glinting in the cold light. You could see the mountain through the smoke from the fields. It did not seem like a good place to go to, yet we were compelled, for here was where the search for divine justice began. The danger of holy places is as nothing compared to when they lie immersed in the poetics of stately being, she was saying, trying to separate her voice from the rasping of frogs squatting in obeisance to the lustrous colors worked by the moon across a flecked sky torn by expectation. Free Fall. The emptiness beneath your feet. That's what I want to tell you about because you live in another time beholden to sacred time but in which the gods have had to disappear into the language itself. . . . I could hear her clicking her fingers like gunshots calling on spirits to detonate the violence of law where death lies enshrined in stately presence, where the taboos, particular histories, and figures of the imagination lie in wait. We have to cross that line she said and never had I seen her so serene and still as she stood there in her thereness. The spirit queen, I mean. Right in the middle of the Three Potencies. It stopped me dead. Was this where my search for divine justice would begin?

— *The Mountain*

It took us the best part of a day. At the top by the side of the stream there was a boulder the size of a house clasped by the roots of a tree. A ladder led from the stream to the top of the boulder on which someone had placed a diminutive sheet of bent-over roofing iron painted with the national colors. Inside burned a candle. A sign suspended from a tree said this was The Palace of the Liberator. Perched so small yet so majestic its claim, its artefactuality emitted a tender radiance.

Behind the boulder a miniature waterfall spurted vigorously between two round stones, glistening with spray. "It's the force of the Liberator," said Ofelia Moscoso, the healer, in her straightforward way, pointing to the water-fall as she laid Haydée down on a flat rock nearby. "Good for business, money, and things to do with government."

Along with millions of cane cutters, ditch diggers, bed-makers, cooks, and house cleaners, Ofelia Moscoso had come to this oil-rich country years ago from the neighbour-ing republic of Costaguana. In colonial times the two countries had been part of the one Vice-Royalty. Now they were fiercely divided,

□ — *The Palace
of the Liberator*

the Costaguanian migrants being labeled with habitual alacrity as thieves and prostitutes, charming testimony to the effervescent logic of taboo and transgression with which world history dedicates the border of the state of the whole to sex and crime.

The Costaguanians would buy forged immigration papers although, truth to tell, it was not that easy to see any difference between doing that and the even more common procedure of "buying" non-forged papers from State officials bribed with the "*tarifa extraoficial*" or *peaje.*

Like the official and the "extra-official," the true and the forged were flip-sides of stately being; neither could exist without the other and this strategic confusion, together with the mystery therein, was dramatically magnified at the border dividing the two republics. What do we mean by "dramatically magnified"? We mean a ritual, but more precisely a literalization, as if staged, of the mystique of sovereignty.

You pass your papers as into a cave at waist height through a semi-circular hole cut into a wall of dark glass. They can see you but you can't see them. And who is looking harder? There is a thump. A primeval force has been disturbed. And it's not so much the rule that has been broken but a matter of knowing the rule or even knowing that there is one. The presence at the other side refuses to reach six inches forward for the papers. They have to be pushed across, deep into the dark womb of official territory known only by the father, possessor of all women, swelling belly and mustache bristling. The tax! The tax! Where's the tax? it bellows. The stupendous brutishness of this desk-thwacking demand announces but one thing: the *tarifa extraoficial*. It seems like the state of the whole has but two discursive speeds: too much or too little. One is grand rhetoric; the other is the silence of the un-sayable, the *tarifa extraoficial*, the un-said that is not so much the limit of language but its presupposition, the spirit queen behind the Liberator.

Ofelia Moscoso was eleven years old when she came and later made a living buying clothes at what are called "duty free" ports, *duty free* being here close cousin to *tarifa extraoficial*. Now she was a healer, of modest pretension, working with the spirits of her new-found land, and here she was by the Liberator's palace getting magic from its state so as to deal with the state. An exile at home with their dead, learning and making it up as she went along, closing the circle on the true and the forged, the official and the extraofficial.

She placed Haydée down on her back, resplendent in her white nightgown there in the forest at the top of the mountain, her red dyed hair falling aflame on the grey rocks, and for the last time put her into trance, beating slowly on a can she found in the profusion of garbage. Haydée lay corpselike for what seemed an eternity inside the tremor of the candles until Ofelia broke the spell by lighting the circle of gunpowder around her. It crackled fiercely. Smoke clung to her red hair, then lifted slowly into the branches to the clear sky beyond.

Ofelia did the same for Haydée's absent husband. She drew an outline of his body on the rocks with talcum powder and placed his shorts and shirt on it. She beat her drum mechanically. Boom. Boom. We waited. Hours seemed to go by. Boom. Boom. The waterfall spurted. Butterflies cavorted. The flames trembled.

We descended slowly, drifting at peace like leaves falling through the jumble of boulders and giant tree trunks, falling like dreams and wraiths of memories and fluttering flags past lonely shrines and remains of altars scattered in the stream's course. There was nobody but us and the souls of the dead. It was mid-week. Ofelia made us bathe in the pools after she'd scattered perfumes over the water — a different perfume for each problem that might befall us in the cruel world below. Translucent fish with black bars running across their backs nibbled at us.

At the bottom of the mountain we forded the river and passed the shacks of the guardians, morose and grudging as ever. Surprised to see us alive? Disappointed that nothing bad had happened? Stupefied with boredom? Eladio waved his stump, all that remained of his right arm. The others sipped at their Pepsi Colas and stared into space, now and again caressing the rotund horizon of their bellies. Pilgrims? They'd seen so many. They'd see them again. Time eternal resting on their vast stomachs rising. Oil out. Cars, ammo, and videos in. The male stomach rising tremulously. Vibrato. The frogs at night in the mud of the canefields behind the shacks under the power line pylons shaking the heavens. The sugarcane mill glowing in the night. The spirit queen calm and aloof on her lake of melted candlewax and cigar butts.

An hour or so later after we'd passed through the town full of immigrants, Italians, Greeks, Portuguese, Palestinians, Spaniards, Lebanese, and a Russian watchmaker, we stood the four of us lonely figures waiting for a bus as cars on important business tore by along the four lane highway stretching majestically to the capital.

Years later I heard of what could happen along that majestic stretch, of the rich young man from the capital who'd for the first time in his life gone to visit the mountain taking his wife and children along with him, at first fascinating, downtrodden people, but wonderfully alive, uplifting, night's falling, getting a little creepy here, how many Indians can you take at one time anyway? And those eyes! Aren't they sort of vacant? And those stomachs! Is that what spirit possession does to you? Are they really needles through the tongue? Let's go. Hop in the Chrysler over the pot holes past the shrine of the *Indio Macho* with the hole chipped into the spirit queen's cunt through the ugly town to reach the freedom of the smooth curves of the highway to the capital . . . and all the time following them this huge truck straight from hell at the back of them no matter how fast they drove. Like a limpet it stuck behind them. Can you imagine? In the night like that? The curves over the deserted hills? The no-man's land of the highway, one of the crueler places on this earth the old sailor would have said, had he lived longer. Forget the serpent-shaped rivers that used to be the highways stretching into the heart of continents. Forget the railroads too, the nineteenth-century scene of lurching shocks rumbling and squealing. All that lies behind in the glare of the lights bearing down as you twist the wheel this way and that as the freeway bores past the shrines to dead truck drivers. Never less than a few inches behind no matter how fast you go. Wouldn't the devil in modern guise be like that? Malevolence in the form of a truck hurtling out of the spirit queen's mountain? Nemesis gathering. Who would tempt fate going to the mountain without someone intimate with the dead? Did they ask permission of the spirit queen? Did they go to the shrines at the entrance to the mountain, the first being the shrine of the *Indio Macho* just outside the gates of the sugar mill, to sit stiller than still smoking *tabacos* reading the signs, cracking their fingers like pistol shots?

It took us the best part of a day. That was in 1983. We had traveled by bus from the capital. Drugged by the afternoon heat and the highway rushing through valleys of peopleless fields dedicated to agribusiness we lost track of time. Oranges in heaps for sale by the side of the road. Polluted lakes. The land baking, never meant to be traversed like this. Two women got in. The driver assured us they would see we got off at the right stop. He knew all about the magic mountain. All about the spirit queen. Indeed as time went by I realized that it was often easiest to talk about her in these casual encounters between strangers passing though moments of controlled intimacy — as in the bus, or in a taxi, at a gas station, in a hotel lobby, at a restaurant, waiting in a queue, on a beach with a stranger. . . . What sort of knowledge is this, you might ask, that in its immense ambivalence trampling the printed page underfoot occupies such a superficial and socially finessed niche wherein it can be not only raised but often — according to its own peculiar rules — explored? But, then, are not the dead the quintessence of stranger-intimacy?

The bus driver had not tried to turn us away — not like the taxi driver in the capital, shaking his head. "Go see the Virgin the other side of the mountains, the national saint," he had implored. He meant the official Virgin, as opposed to the spirit queen, the "extra-official" one, and he was more than scared. Mere mention of this specter plummeted him into abjection. Most everywhere you got that feeling. Rich people as scared as poor people. Maybe more so. Stories of strange disappearances and labyrinthine underground chambers dedicated to human sacrifice, yes, Sir! And even stranger visitations of scurrilous spirits in the beds of pubescent girls and stories of brutal murder, picked up as children from their maids or from the grandparents. Embellished by the telling, these circulating images blended fear and fascination with some unnameable restraint pitchforking thought into a vacuum of silence at the center of language itself. But none of this perturbed our bus driver or our new-found friend, Ofelia, calm and smiling emissary of fate.

We got off by the side of the highway and walked under the bridge into the town sloping downhill with its pastry shops, clothes stores, haberdashery, liquor store, magic shops, modern church, and plaza with the statue of the Liberator around which men stood in small groups, clutching at their manhood. As far as the eye could see there were one and two-story drab concrete buildings festooned with electric wires and cables, together with cars circling and a few bedraggled taxis waiting to take people to the mountain. Ofelia plunged into one of those splendid shops of magical supplies with which the country is abundantly endowed and which for some curious reason are called *perfumeries*. She bought candles for the colors of the national flag, red, blue, and yellow, and white ones as well. She bought talcum powder, flowers, and bottles of essences for business, for luck, for money, and for opening the way.

These essences have been licensed for sale and production as "cosmetics" by the state of the whole since 1985, and maybe some such historically contingent fact helps explain why these stores dispensing magic on a national scale are called or continued to be called *perfumeries* — the term being akin, as a state-endorsed deceit, to "duty-free port" or *tarifa extraoficial*. These terms are exemplary of that wonderful phenomenon wherein what is opposed to the rigor of Law partakes of its language and power, the *tarifa extraoficial*, for instance, belonging both to the world of officialdom and to a burlesque of that world in its meaning an illegal bribe that is so routinized that it is essential to governing. What brings this into the orbit of the magic of the state, of course, in concert with the trickery involved by mimesis and alterity, is the simultaneous admission and negation of this otherwise glaring but necessary contradiction. For corruption to be maintained as an open secret at this intensity there has to be a stout denial that it occurs. It completely misses the point to say that the state is corrupt, because for corruption to be systematic there has to exist its systematic opposite, the rule of Law — and at the center of this turbulence we can already see the methodical figure of Ofelia stooping over Haydée's prone body dressed in flowing white by the Palace of the Liberator by the side of the waterfall spurting between glistening boulders.

"Ah yes! 1985. That was the year," Señora Bolívar was saying in reference to the year the state made magical essences legal merchandise, classifying them as cosmetics. She was tiny, dressed in white, elegantly seated in a large wicker chair, fanning herself in the sultry evening air. She owned and managed a small factory that made magical essences in the back rooms of her home many miles away to the west in the densely settled hills above a vast polluted lake. Before 1985, she said, police would harass her trucks pounding across the republic. The base of the essences came from France and was dreadfully expensive, she explained, but now many manufactures just bottle colored water. Even the magical essence business, it appears, suffers from corruption and fraud. The whole country is going to hell not in a basket but in a bottle of magical essence. "This business is all ticket," she kept saying. "All ticket." By which she meant the labeling, and she got one of her beautiful daughters to drag forth a precious scrapbook of labels she had used since she got into the business in the early 1970s. And she laughed. It was intensely amusing. "All ticket," she kept giggling. But she takes pride in turning out a good product. It was a condition of legalization to have her work checked regularly by the state, which sent an expert for that purpose. "Of course it was a political appointment," she said, eyes smiling, "and the *doctora* turned out to know nothing. We had to teach her." The demand for her product is too large for her to keep up. There are perfumeries all over

the country that she has to supply. Some buy the entire truck-load! Orders even come from Costaguana and Miami.

The perfumery we were in with Ofelia and Haydée sold essences for a pretty substantial spectrum of human hopes and despairs, together with powders and a vast number of images and different sorts of liquor. The *indios* only go for local and cheap drink and you can see the Indians on the labels on the bottles. The *Vikingos* go for expensive foreign drinks, like whisky, as does the Liberator, because although he's from here he is a deeply respected figure. With him you can only drink from a small spirit glass; never directly from the bottle. But most of the shelves and display cases were given over to statues and portraits of the spirit queen, the Liberator, *Negro* Felipe, *Negro* Primero, *Negra* Matea, the Solitary Soul (the *Anima Sola*), the long dead dictator Juan Vicente Gómez, in uniform, just the head and upper chest, the soul of the Desertor of Guengue, also very spooky,

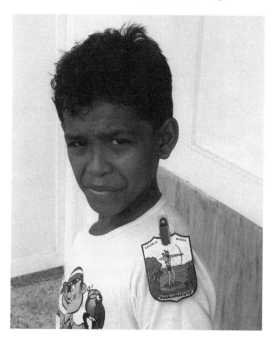

the good-hearted medical doctor José Gregorio, the Fragment of the Testament of the Liberator, US Plains Indians with magnificent war bonnets, a fat Bhudda smiling, a couple of Vikings, and many, but many, heads of wild Indians with terrible grimaces.

"One of the tough guys," responded a ten-year-old boy weeks later when I showed him a medallion that I had bought, the size of a thumbnail with the picture of one of these fierce heads.

On the front of the medallion was an Indian in delicate pastels. But on the back was an embossed outline of Jesus. No color. Just indentations.

Jesus. On the back?

What's happened to the good old days? Then when you read about *syncretism* in a European Elsewhere it was the other way around, Jesus up front and the pagan gods hidden behind. Now if Jesus had been done away with, that I'd understand. It's putting him behind that unsettles.

A behind Jesus?

Do they secretly worship Jesus now, behind a pagan front?

Ofelia spent a heap of money on flowers and essences, at least a week's wages. She made us each buy a Cross of Caravaca to hang around our neck for protection as we approached the mountain. The cord by which the cross was suspended was plaited from the national colors. There were arm bands and belts woven of the national colors too. All for protection.

But why did we need so much protection and what was it we were being protected from?

Together with the multicolored profusion of images and statues, perfumes and powders, there was a solitary book for the equivalent of 45 US dollars by the Cuban (later exile), Lydia Cabrera, first published in Havana in 1948. Entitled *El monte* which, given the book's content, could be translated as "the sacred forest" as well as "the mountain," it was an impressive scholarly study of Afro-Cuban rituals garnering power from the forest — or rather the power flowing from the attribution of magical force to the forest as a metaphor for that nether-world beyond and defining the Euro-colonial city and its civilization. But who could buy it at that price, wild as it was?

The opening paragraph read as follows: "Belief in the spirituality of the *monte* persists among black Cubans with astonishing tenacity. In the forests and thickets of Cuba, there live on, as in the jungles of Africa, the same ancestral deities and powerful spirits that still today are feared and worshipped, and on whose hostility or benevolence depend one's successes or failures."

Night was falling as our taxi approached the looming bulk of the mountain. The road changed to dirt and potholes with a well-maintained drain on either side. It was roofed over by branches of *mataretón* trees with barbed wire tacked to their trunks behind which the prehistoric forms of cattle grazed, profiled against the forest of sugarcane. Ofelia was happy and alert. She asked if I wanted a cigar.

No!

Don't you want to learn witchcraft? asked the taxidriver.

Who asked him anyway?

No! I already know.

Well. Here's a chance to learn a little more, he chuckled. (Oh! These taxi drivers driving you anywhere, telling you everything.)

A few days ago, he went on, a group of thirty pilgrims were robbed blind. Lost everything on the mountain. He was enjoying himself. You can't be too careful. . . . And here he was taking us into the abyss. They'll drive you anywhere. Tell you anything.

It was a half hour ride. We passed the shrine of the *Indio Macho* at the entrance to the sugar mill. Cars were parked. Candles were alight in the shrine. People were standing by, smoking *tabacos*, gulping the smoke in great gasps of spiritual hunger and reading the ash for the sign that permission to proceed onward to the mountain was granted. The shrine of the *Indio Macho* was a sort of Immigration Control.

And behind the shrine were the twinkling lights of the mill with the smoke from its immense chimney drawing out the darkness flung across the sky.

It was strange but in all my trips to the mountain since 1983 I don't think I once saw a person or a vehicle go in or out of the entrance to the sugar mill. It was as if the mill ran itself.

Years later alone with Virgilio nursing his tired old taxi over the pot-holes at night with a *ranchero* wailing in the arthritic tape deck it struck me that there was a spiritual affinity between the mill and the mountain despite their appearing quite different from one another — the mountain being all fable, the mill harshly real, albeit with twinkling lights, working incessantly twenty-four hours a day. The workers even worked Christmas day. They were burning canefields on Good Friday. They never let up.

Perhaps what I discerned was that mill and mountain served to reflect each other and thereby bring out something otherwise inaccessible and important in each other, the interesting and maybe important thing being that while the mountain, of course, leapt forth as a brilliant work of the imagination, a spectacle and awesome work of art, the lofty sugar mill at its base did not at first glance appear that way at all. Instead it appeared as something natural or at least something mundane, secular, and taken for granted. While nature was celebrated on the mountain as part of the enchanted domain of the spirit queen, mistress of the serpents and dragons, the sugar mill was natural in that it belonged to utility, efficiency, the world of wage labor and modern commerce. But then you started to sense something else going on with the mill — perhaps because of the sharpness of its juxtaposition with this mist-laden mountain dedicated to profitless expenditure. For the mountain emitted a contagion across the boundaries set by the river, the wavy line of sugarcane, and the high-voltage pylons strung along its base. Its presence hung as a pall pulsating across the countryside and right there as if preordained where all the world passed through Immigration Control to get to the mountain, right there at the point defined by the shrine of the *Indio Macho* and the entrance to the mill, the mountain demanded payment. For the owner of the mill, the Cuban, has a contract with the spirit queen: she demands human life, otherwise production comes to a standstill.

Take the people at the settlement of Aguas Negras, twenty-five miles away at the end of a road of mud in an ocean of sugarcane:

neat wooden houses, a cinder-block school with colored murals of the Liberator and scenes depicting the anti-colonial wars, all in the officially contrived naive and "childish" style. It's occupied mainly by migrants, black cane cutters from the adjoining republic of poverty and violence, men, sometimes with their families, all the way from the fast-flowing rivers and jungles of the Pacific coast. "My dad would never work for the mill near the mountain," says the young girl, "'cos the spirit queen demands the life of a worker every three months." It's the first thing they'll tell you about the spirit queen. That's what she means to them. And not much more. I've known some of these people since 1969, years before they crossed that border.

Then there was Luís Manuel Castillo born by the sea in the hottest of towns some forty miles away. He is seventy-four years old and lives alone as caretaker of a small farm in the hills a few miles north of the mountain. A green nylon hammock in the corner and a few cardboard boxes for furniture. He said he first heard of the spirit queen when he was twenty-two, working as a laborer for the Department of Public Works. People told him her contract with the Cuban owner of the sugar mill required one dead worker a week! That was in 1940.

He remembered a man who was paid a generous wage to paint the smokestack of the mill. Each day they would see him, heroically inching up like a moth emerging from its chrysalis, transforming the smokestack beneath him. He reached the top. He swayed on the rim, lost his balance and fell in. Burnt to a char. A moth in the flame.

Ten years ago a different story started to circulate, according to Luís Manuel, that the spirit queen no longer wanted the souls of the humble who, after all, were merely doing what they had to do to provide for themselves and their families.

Now she wanted the soul of the owner himself.

The story wants to tell us something. It is like a visiting card from the future and certainly from fate, a sign thrown up by history as to a possible change in course, a cipher bobbing in the entrails of envy and class war. A man falls into the furnace of industrious industry and is consumed as in sacrifice. And now she wants the owner himself? Climbing alone, silhouetted against sky and mountain. The heat of the sun. The swirling rain and mist. The heat of the furnace. A heroic figure. Inching upwards. The paint spreading neatly below. The vertiginous fall into the solar anus.

Luís Manuel looked extremely healthy despite what the young boys in town whose father owns the farm he caretakes say about peasants.

There he is with his shirt off, straw hat, grinning, big chest, swinging his machete.

"They work too hard and that's why they get sick."

"They walk too much and get doubled over 'cos they carry such heavy weights."

Worlds divided by speed, by weight, by walking, and by generation. Cars, ammo, and videos in. Two worlds held together by the spirit queen. For the boys spend a lot of time hanging out by the shacks at the base of the mountain. They learn a lot of stuff from spirit-medium women. They hang out with the son of one of the most important spirit-mediums of the mountain. She is rich now. Her son drives into the nearby city and brings boys home at night for his pleasure. They know the big car thieves who cruise through town, buy their way out of gaol, and work with the criminal court, the *Corte Malandra*, one of the most powerful if least-known courts that the spirit queen has, composed of criminals who were killed by the police and helped the poor. Chavo Fredy, Chavo Ismael, for instance. Their chiefs are Pedro Sánchez and Luís Segundo. In Quiballo at the foot of the mountain there are quite a few people who work with them. People visit their graves in the capital too. There are as far as I know no images of these spirits. Which is strange.

The rain set in. We fell asleep in the green hammock. Every now and again Luís Manuel would dip his little finger into a tiny can with a black sticky substance in it. "It's tobacco," he said. "Nicotine paste. Lots of peasants around here use it. You can buy it anywhere."

Like the cigars used with such relish by the pilgrims who travel to the mountain from all over the country, so here there was this emphatic trace of a pre-Colombian world — as we read about it. Who can forget the ritual use of *tabacos* (plural) reported for the Caribbean and surrounding *Tierra Firme* by Oviedo as far back as the early sixteenth century, or the current tobacco inhalation by the shamans and sorcerers of the Orinoco delta? But now with the pilgrim it was a trace in substance, not in meaning. Nobody sucking on their *tabaco* thought of it as indigenous, let alone as an indigenously "sacred" substance. Curious. The most indigenous thing about these enthusiasts of the Indian flocking to the spirit queen's mountain was a substance whose indigenous significance was lost to consciousness. Does this sacrifice to history point to the limitations or strengths of a materialist historiography? Does sacrifice entail here identification with the being that is killed, a split consciousness that not only dies but confronts death and revels in it? Would this be the root of the obsession not only with the dead but with *tabaco*, smoke curling, head spinning, continuously reading the language-signs twirling in the ash, these strange correspondences brought into being with the after-life of the *tabaco*?

The taxi passed through walls of cane. Not a breath of wind. At the end of the road were half a dozen makeshift tin sheds. The driver took his money and left in a swirl of dust. Maybe *he* didn't want to learn about witchcraft either. A greying man with a stump for an arm wearing a singlet came out and greeted Ofelia as "Sister." As if determined to further our anxiety, he advised us to forget about sleeping on the mountain because of thieves and murderers lurking there. Paranoiac and know-all he gazed at the hazy horizon and waved his stump to indicate where he had recently seen a suspicious bunch of people. His words were lost in the cacophany of frogs which, with the setting of the sun, began to fill the darkening dome of the world.

Above, the cold silhouette of the mountain. Around us, smoke exhaled by a bunch of bare-chested men dressed in shorts puffing furiously and spitting, each an effigy of compacted concentration, scrupulously examining the ash as they twirled their cigars between their fingers at the foot of a statue of the spirit queen.

Down the road, just beyond a long shelter for hanging hammocks, was another shrine. In it stood a statue of the spirit queen side by side with the Liberator, the national flag, the grimacing head of the *Indio* Guaicaipuro, a black and white drawing of a rather sad looking Professor Lino Valle, the learned hermit of the mountain, now dead, and several plaques bearing messages like "Thank you *Negro* Felipe" and "Gratitude and Admiration to the Liberator for Favors Granted."

We felt trapped between the mountain and these guardians prowling and praying. Why were they here? Why were we? What did they do? One of them emerged from a partitioned off cubicle at the back of the shed, a startlingly obese and dour man aged about thirty-five, in tight shorts, a large crucifix hanging between sweaty breasts. They called him Zambrano. Back in there he had a dirty hammock next to a shrine made of statues of the Three Potencies floating on clouds of candlewax and funeral pyres of cigar butts and ash.

He came from the capital. He had a studious, professorial air about him. That first night his lover, a young man from the neighbouring republic, unschooled, lean and handsome, told me they had just returned from Haiti where Zambrano had been studying voodoo. He's a *brujo*, he added. Years later Virgilio told me he was a powerful healer and a good guy. He was a touch too fanatical for me but years later we made real contact. It was hard to figure out what kept him going.

He asked us if we knew what the spirit queen was all about, and took us outside behind the shed on the edge of the canefield. The stars were out. He said this mountain was for the people of this country like the wailing wall was for the Jews. Here you purified your spirit in communion with the spirit queen. His voice trembled between a command and an appeal. She had been the daughter of the indigenous ruler of these parts. The Europeans killed him then turned on the daughter who escaped into the wilderness. No one ever came across her remains. Now she lives on in the mountain, ruler of the animals, the serpents and dragons, as well as of the spirits of the dead humans that history composts here. It's the Indians, he insisted, the Indians are the primary source of spiritual regeneration of the nation. That's the reason, that's the force, which brings people to the mountain!

Rising behind him in the shadows absorbing his tale, the mountain seemed bigger than its history. The place had an atmosphere of its own for which the history was mere caption.

Years later Katy told me different. That the spirit queen was not an Indian but a *mestiza*, hybrid child of an Indian woman and a *conquistador* (sixteenth century) and that she had had to seek refuge in the mountain until saved by the Liberator (born late eighteenth century) who sent *el Negro* Felipe to care for her.

But to the lanky dark-skinned man who walked all day back and forth along the sand by the far-off ocean selling oysters beyond the capital city — "Buy your *Vitamina C*, Get the Shine in your Eyes, *Vitamina C*!" — the spirit queen, whom he adored, had no particular "racial" identity. No! She was not Black, not White, not Indian, nor any mixture thereof. Instead, he paused, she *was* the nation. It was that simple. What's more, her father was a vagabond. Her mother used to beat her. And one day she disappeared, taken away by the water spirits, known as *encantados*.

But where, then, was she now, this taken-away creature, meandering if not lost in the realm of the *encantados*? And what did such a fate imply for the nation? His eyes shone at the thought of it.

All this would have been, I fear, lost on the fat man, Zambrano. For his was a tragic tale soaked in the drama of Indians and conquest, death and resurrection of the nation as woman in a wrenching turnabout of fate. He shook his head at the wonder and the beauty of it all. Unlike many of the pilgrims torn by a proximate despair, he lived here. For he was a visionary and a devotee. Year in, year out, I saw him there, the unmoved mover getting fatter and fatter, unshaven, wiping the sweat off his glasses. I doubt if he ever set foot beyond the confines of his shed with its acrid cigar smoke and the Three Potencies, calm as could be, wreathed in the mystery of race, sex, and the seductive violence of stories of colonial conquest. He would stare out for hours, resting his bespectacled head on his elbows, staring at the pilgrims coming and going in their cars and hired buses. Did he know what Luís Manuel Castillo knew, I wondered? And if he did, was that what kept him here?

3 — *The Shrines*

At daybreak we forded the river, leaving the
guardians asleep with their troubled dreams
in the lands of the dead by plaster-of-paris
statues and tobacco smoke trailing though
histories, epic and familiar, where the state
of the whole edged over into brilliant displays
of sacral discharge. Someone screamed. A
lizard was hacked with a machete, head rearing, clawing at the earthen floor. Someone
plucked at a guitar. Sleep was in a far away
place where the living and the dead lay neatly
divided.

We waded the river and entered the forest. Not a sound. The trees formed pale
columns between which we passed like
shadows in single file on well trod soil. How
many people had passed before? Years later
Virgilio said that when he first went to the
mountain, in the early 1940s, there were but
three Virgins and no other statues, no
Indians, no Africans, and no city people. In
those days there was no spirit possession
either. Just voices. When Lino Valle, Virgilio's
godfather, the hermit who lived in the mountain, cured people, he would solicit voices
from these trees.

Oh Apóstol de la Diosa de la Montaña; tú que sembraste la primera semilla de la fraternidad venezolana en el Paraíso encantado de la Diosa verdadera de nuestros antepasados, tú que con sublime dignidad reviviste la tradición sagrada.

Oh santificado espíritu del profesor LINO VALLES, sé nuestro protector, como primer Apóstol que eres de la Reina María Lionza. Amén.

(Se reza un padrenuestro y se limpia uno con su esencia especial).

□ —— *Lino Valle*

A wan light filtered through the canopy of branches. Now and again we saw dirty plastic sheets tied between trees — pilgrims, Ofelia said, as she hurried along. But it was mid-week and nobody was visible, the pilgrims coming mainly on weekends or national holidays. The solitude was immense. Just the scream of mosquitoes in this mournful wood and the rustle of falling leaves.

Now and again we came across white powder marks on the earth and empty liquor bottles by cairns of stones at the foot of a tree. Sometimes the powder marks took the form of a blurred outline of a human body, other times they formed baroque geometrical designs like hieroglyphs framing the remains of candles, rotting fruit, and flowers. Vestiges of *portales*, Ofelia explained. *Portal.* It was the first time I'd heard the word and it had a curious ring. It literally means an entrance, gateway, or hall. Here it meant a shrine or altar. *But what do I mean by "literally"?* By being called a gateway, the notion of a shrine acquired unexpected meaning.

For the newcomer whose unaccustomed ear discerns the freshness of metaphor, providing through the juxtaposition of images the entrance to a new world, the *portal* itself was more than an apt metaphor joining *gateway* to *shrine*. It was beyond perfection, the image, indeed the metaphor, of metaphor itself, no less than its stunning literalization — a wondrous metaphor-machine designed to set the scene of spirit passing into body, possession as embodiment activating images made precious by death and stately remembrance.

Nietzsche made the point that metaphor constitutes the human world by being forgotten, absorbed in the cultural reality it forms as literal truth. "Truths are illusions of which one has forgotten that they *are* illusions; worn-out metaphors which have become powerless to affect the senses; coins which have their obverse effaced and now are no longer of account as coins but merely as metal." Reality is a sort of conjuring trick whereby poetic illumination flares for the moment only to pass into routine, engorged with value by virtue of this vanishing act. Might it not be the singular holiness of a *portal*, therefore, to resurrect this abysmal valuation?

We entered a clearing flooded with light to come face to face with the first active *portal*, that of the Red Indian.

It was a beautiful shrine, a diorama of the state as a work of art, condensing its magic into one explosive montage. A bucolic North American plains Indian in war bonnet stood astride a toy theater of the state complete with the national flag, a bronze-colored bust of the Liberator and the split head of the spirit queen, crown intact. A crumpled image of the wounded and (hence) blessed Hand of Jesus with a saint emerging from each fingertip completed this toy-theater tableau over all of which, in stirring color and the vigor of youth, presided yet another portrait of the Liberator painted into the national flag to form a magnificent backdrop.

I thought of the medallions, the Indian on front, Christ behind, for here too, as a gateway to magical powers, the Indian serenely dwarfed the sacred hand of the Nation-State in its crypt below.

Haydée placed four bottles of urine on the portal. From friends of hers.

Ofelia placed an offering of an orange cut into quarters, together with candles of the national colors and three types of liquor in plastic cups. She sat down in front of the *portal* for a few minutes, concentrating, smoking a cigar, clicking her fingers, "looking for obstacles." When the ash of the cigar showed everything clear she began to cure or, as she put it, she began to work.

In front of the *portal* she sprinkled talcum powder to make a life-sized outline of the human form into which she placed Haydée, face upwards. Around her she placed five cups of liquor and 24 candles and when they were lit — an impressive sight — she began to beat on an old tin can she found in the rubbish amid discarded cans of pop, cartons of cooking oil and juice, plastic cups, old flowers, darting humming birds, butterflies, and, according to the wind, odors of human shit.

Within her circle of flame Haydée, still as a corpse and deathly pale, closed her eyes while Ofelia kept drumming.

Out of nowhere a tall angular Black man with a drum and a sword, or was it a wand, leapt like a dancing spider into the clearing. Out of nowhere without a sound. He put the point of the sword over Haydée's head, blessed her with the sign of the Cross, and rapidly in a high-pitched mechanical tone recited an invocation to

- the Celestial Court
- the Medical Court
- the African Court
- the Indian Court.

Ofelia kept on drumming as if absolutely nothing had happened.

The man with the sword (or was it a wand?) leapt and disappeared bounding up the rocks and over fallen tree trunks. Was he real? Up high was a group of people he was accompanying. A woman yelled down angrily. "Crossed! Crossed!" I had crossed my arms.

Haydée lay unmoved under the spell of the *portal*. Later she said she was conscious of all that had happened. Perhaps just as the spidery man had danced out of the forest to bless her with his invocations, so too figures from the *portal* had emerged from the death-space of the *portal* to dance and to bless her?

"How much time's gone by?" asked Ofelia in a tired and bored voice.

"About ten minutes."

"Another ten, then," she said resignedly. Her fingertips hurt. The sun was climbing. We were tired having barely slept.

After Haydée walked out of the circle backwards, I asked Ofelia what had been going on and she told me that the spirit of the Indian had been entering. The drumming is to invoke the Indian. The drumming is to give light, she said.

Hijacked from the great plains of the imperial imagination, drawn from another history of the brave circulating in the minds of the victors, this U.S. Plains Indian bore the brunt of primitivism — to testify to and draw out the otherwise inarticulable magic and sacred design of the modern state. The image of the Indian was a key, so to speak, a key to the state's sacred interior, to the theater of its sacred hand now extended towards a possessable populace. It was the sacred interior we find in the modern state, the spirit queen, unsettling Kafka's Castle. . . . "It was late in the evening when K. arrived. The village was deep in snow. The Castle hill was hidden, veiled in mist and darkness, nor was there even a glimmer of light to show that a castle was there. On the wooden bridge leading from the main road to the village K. stood for a long time gazing into the illusory emptiness above him." In the perfumeries you buy images of the spirits. Some are laminated in plastic like the state-issued Identity Cards mandatory even for children and, like credit cards, designed to slip into a wallet. On the back are prayers to the spirit-saint to be read aloud. It seems maybe that Kafka had something like these prayers in mind when he wrote some of his "aphorisms" and "parables," like *The Wish To Be A Red Indian* on a racing horse leaning against the wind quivering over the quivering ground until the horse's head disappeared together with the ground itself. He'll show you round, this postmodern brave slipping south easily over borders to find new resting places in the happy hunting grounds where civilization daily confronts its savagery. A match made in heaven, the ethereal confluence of reason and violence within the state; the constitution of its very being. This mortal god, Hobbes said, and rightfully so, for what else but a certain brand of holiness could hold together in the wound of the one stigmatized hand the promise of justice and the monopoly of the legitimate use of violence as well?

"How long have I been drumming?" asked Ofelia. Haydée was in another world. Like a corpse in her circle of flame. The sun was getting hotter.

He'll show you 'round, this sweet brave. He's got what it takes these days to trigger the finger-snapping release of negation as holy-being, the *work*, as Ofelia insists on calling it, the finger-snapping work of the negative; a saint for each fingertip, the Indian above, the Liberator and the spirit queen below; Haydée stretched out as we in our watching complete the spiritual embodiment; Ofelia drumming her fingers off. For light. For death. For the work of the spirit (wrote Hegel) "endures death and in death maintains its being. It only wins to truth when it finds itself utterly torn asunder. It is this mighty power only by looking the negative in the face and dwelling within it." But Hegel didn't know the extent to which he was right (says Bataille). He saw labor, the labor of the negative, when he should have also seen play. And Hegel has nothing to say about sex.

All that day we went up the mountain following the stream bed by the side of which, like so many pearls threaded on a string, were different *portales*, or remains thereof, cunningly inserted into crevices, twisted roots, and clefts in rock faces, as if nature was asking humanity to interpose an image so as to complete a sign. Now and again there would be a pool strewn with boulders around which we made our way. Sometimes the boulders were painted with the national colors.

We climbed like sleepwalkers, dulled by the heat, yet apprehensive. Even frightened. Of what I do not know. Some power which in its ritual genius allows unconscious things to surface, enriching the mind, while still maintaining the law against those things? There had to be an architect responsible for the layout of this massive spirit-theater. But plainly there was none. It was against architecture. But could something like this anarchic hallowed ground cut into civil society just emerge on its own, siphoning off the spirit-power of the state? Or were we afraid of thieves, looking up at unexpected sounds? Killers perhaps? Difficult not to be, after the dire warnings of the guardians.

But something else was brooding in those warnings, something more than thieves and rapists and assassins — a surplus of inarticulable danger intimated by those figures but extending way beyond them, disrupting questions of cause and effect. If thieves and murderers truly existed here, did this mean they were the cause of the fear, or did it mean there was something about the mountain which attracted them hither, drawn as moths to a flame to commit their crimes and fortify the mountain's holiness?

This danger cannot be named. But that is the least of it. The *portal* gathers this danger in the urge to completion of a sign begun by nature opening into the earth of the mountain reaching to the sky. By definition a *portal*, a gateway, is always open, a wound, never a resolution.

And now we see Haydée inert as unto death spread forth below the Liberator and the spirit queen, serene in the death-space of their underworld beneath the Indian brave swept off the great plains, the nation's colors flaring, Haydée entranced, Ofelia drumming, the man leaping into the circle from nowhere with the sword that is a wand to touch her lightly, invoking the courts of the queen.

This leap from nowhere is contagious. A line of flight. It moves us too, beginning with the understanding that the need to participate in the storm is an end in itself and no less pressing than the need to exploit the mountain's magic so as to resolve the burdensome issues of the everyday. It is this passion, ultimately, that is the danger generated by the mountain, threatening to diffuse beyond its base, sweeping across the river, past the corrugated iron sheds of the guardians, past one-armed Eladio pointing paranoiacally with his stump, past lonely Zambrano vacant-eyed and shrewd, hunched over his cigar, past the *portal* of the *Indio Macho* by the gates to the sugar mill, past all these sentinels and gateways so as to enter the freeways sweeping majestically to the capital.

This leap from nowhere with the sword that is a wand is the leap that combines violence with holiness, spasmodically recharging the circulation of power between the dead and the living, the state and the people. Here where the body becomes the stage of nothingness upon which the great drama of stately forms can parade alongside rampant impulse and aborted signification, where disembodiment gives way to other embodiments secreting magical force, here is the scene of the "gateway," the *portal*, serene in the necessity of its mission impossible. And this is why this danger cannot be named. Instead it leaks. As into these very words. It can be neither contained nor structured no matter how severe the dualisms, no matter how formalized the law. And this is why the last gasp effort, the *portal* exists, and is beautiful and powerful. For the *portal* is the effort of containment, of repeated and glorious failure, intimation of containment where constellations of imagery figuring and refiguring the state of the whole pass through slow release wave-impulses of ritual to cross the threshold separating the living from the dead.

Right there, pin-pointed in the *portal*, the gateway, the great metaphor-machine oscillating back and forth between literality and figure in the flare and disappearance of poetry into truth no less than of spirit into body is where sign and substance, the state and the people, for one prolonged, gratifying and alchemical instant, fuse. This is what, I guess, Zambrano, feels, year in, year out, head cupped between his hands, candles flaring in pools of wax at the feet of the queen in the obscurity of his shack, what Eladio waves his stump at, shadowy dangers stalking the horizon of the cane fields, and what Ofelia and Haydée jointly create as the Indian brave looks down upon the toy theater of the Liberator and the spirit queen, diorama of the state of the whole.

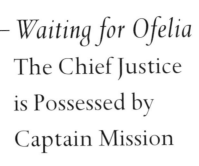

4 — *Waiting for Ofelia*
The Chief Justice
is Possessed by
Captain Mission

It was never like that again, not in all the years he returned after 1983. He kept waiting for Ofelia to make it right again, something honest and straightforward, enigmatic and powerful, beautiful and laced with humor. Just two gentle ladies and two *gringos* on their way elsewhere, picked up in a bus mainlining for the magic mountain to extract a smidgin of power from the state of the whole on a quiet weekday. But no matter how many times he went back he never found her. Once the guardians told him she'd been by. Another time he wrote, but there was no reply. Chances were the letter never even got there. He went and tried to find her at the address she'd given at the edge of the city:

```
Fifth Drainage Ditch
House #DDT 18
Valencia
```

But even though they'd spent the night there after the visit to the mountain, he couldn't locate the house.

What had seemed then like a chapter out of a fairy story, calmly unfolding by means of shrines ascending to the Liberator's palace on the mountain's peak, turned out, on later visits, to be an exception. What usually happened was very different. The elements remained the same but the overall effect was something else.

From the farthest reaches of the country, people came on weekends and national holidays in what they called missions or caravans of anything from three to thirty people under the leadership of one person. They would set up camp in the mountain, but usually not more than a half mile from the river. In the camp site they would build their *portal* and rarely venture beyond. These camps were usually of plastic sheeting and when there were many they composed something like a medieval city of narrow streets twisting between glistening walls at times white and opaque, at times semi-translucent, depending on the light and time of day. At night from the outside you could see the glowing colors of the *portal* together with the moving forms of people in the great scenes of possession. Other times people would allow their plastic "theaters" to open partially to passers-by such that, taken as a whole, it was not unlike a medieval fairground with glistening scene after scene, possession after possession, shone dully as so many overlays into the one plastic mass swaying delicately under the trees at the base of the mountain. It is the plastic realm shuddering and mobile that lies densely before and within us.

Taking priority over the original.

Plastic spirits, plastic cities, malleable and ripping in the wind.

Colored lights and movement filter through the body alight with translucence.

While spirits dance in from Cuba via Miami via Italian emigrant-owned plaster of paris factories working overtime in the slums of the third world megalopolis, this century now, the malleable spirit century spread across her glistening sea, the plastic realm.

Blue shards of plastic snagged by trees along the river banks in the isolated forests of the Pacific Coast, green forest, blue

flapping blue

jerking vortices of tearing

in the ferocious currents of the earth-filled water, gold mines above, slave labor below. Timbiqui. Here at the end of the earth the plastic realm.

A beautiful deep blue, the blue of heaven beckoning between frenzies.

Orange plastic. Black plastic. And white plastic bags tearing on barbed wire screaming the night long across the wind-whipped empty sands of the Guajira peninsula reaching out into sea, here on delicately heaving dunes under cold stars, orange ones, black ones, white ones.

The white line, the white line of plastic now part of nature, "second nature," the plastic realm shuddering and mobile before and within us stretching due north along the Yucatan high-water mark further than any eye can see together with drift-wood and sea-weed marking the swelling mass of ocean,

rising, subsiding,

nature's turnabout and extremity in the long white line

counterbalancing the drift of tides and moon swinging, swinging over the glistening mass of Carib sea, the spirit queen's home of homes. *Queen of harvests and waters . . .* and of human extremity, dragons and serpents, cities of plastic without toilets or garbage facility, holiness rising on this incandescent ferment of human necessity keeping watch through the night and the following night and all nights hereafter.

Of sleep there would be little, the night propitious for visitations by spirits, while during the heat of the tropical day the plastic encumbered atmosphere was stupefyingly soporific, no matter how bold the images, dramatic the action. The clearly etched spirit-images dribbled into lethargic banality punctuated by frenzied outbursts as the possessions fired or misfired taking off in unanticipated directions.

He lived, then, for years, oscillating between these two layers of experience, first time and other times, narrative and abandon, redemption and abjection, unable to adjust one to the other, waiting for what memory portrayed as an ever-increasing perfection of the first time to reassert itself, waiting, that is, for Ofelia to retrieve the souful mix of light-hearted common sense and humor that was sorely lacking.

There was the shock when he was accused of *obscure works* by the Black Cuban. It was Christmas Day. Someone came to Katy's camp saying there was a man dressed in a wig by the *portal* at the end of the path by the field of sugarcane talking like an old lady. Lots of people were watching. Someone else said that the man was talking English and was angry. It was late afternoon. There was a dark-skinned man in shorts strutting back and forth in front of the *portal*. He had no shirt, lots of beads and crucifixes around his neck, and a floppy felt hat. Katy said it was the spirit of the Black Cuban. Another man, also just in shorts, with a huge pot belly, was holding his arms outstretched like a shield over the Black Cuban's head, quivering, "with the force." A young woman dressed as an "Indian" was standing to one side, shaking, with a glazed expression. She had a headband of the national colors. People were seated on a bench watching the Black Cuban, and behind them were still more people. It was the theater of possession. The man's eyes. Rolling. His strange speech. Crouching movements. Stick-like gesticulations. Grotesque twisting inwards of the elbows, wrists, and knees. The crowd very much part of it too, spellbound, yet also judgmental and a little skeptical. There was an air of lethargic routine to it all. They clapped at the end. A show. Was there an end?

Katy's daughter encouraged him to step forward and receive the spirit's blessing. He could help cure you, perhaps. Give you good advice, perhaps. Many people were doing this but he felt shy and vulnerable. Katy's boyfriend, Francesco, stepped forward to be blessed. The Black Cuban had a lot to say but it was hard to follow as his supposedly English speech was slurred Spanish. Katy looked on with a bemused smile. A little too bemused. When they walked away she said the Black Cuban had accused him of "working in obscurity," working with malign spirits. His stomach tightened. How do you respond to an accusing spirit? Had his sense of vulnerability betrayed him?

"I don't think he's right," went on Katy, "but tomorrow I want to give you a bath." She told him he needed the spirit of the "medical court" which includes the spirit of doctor José Gregorio Hernández. She could be transported by any one of these.

But later on lying back in her nylon hammock she declared the guy was faking.

Her daughter, smoking cigars, was preparing a stocky man for purification in front of their little *portal*. "Preparing the material." Placing the person face up in a circle of candles in front of a *portal*, concentrating quietly by his side, purifying the body, making it more able to be one day possessed — "transported" they say — by wholesome spirits. She was only seventeen and so confident. Only a few days before, her mother said proudly, she had been possessed for the first time! Possessed by an Indian. Nameless.

Francesco was driving Katy in from the city two hours away most every weekend at that time. They were among the privileged few who had a permanent site on the flat land above the river adjacent to the parking lot and the tin sheds of the vacant-eyed guardians. Sometimes she would stay the week with one or the other of her daughters and Francesco would come out on the weekend in his beat-up van when the factory shift was over. She was forty years old and had seven children. Like Ofelia, she was serene. She sat around most of the time with a blasé smile on her face and nothing much to say except how beautiful it was that everyone called each other brother and sister and how beautiful the mountain was, as she whacked at the mosquitoes. Her hair was cut short and dyed blonde and she had beautiful peachlike, golden-brown skin. Her smile was not only constant but a little unnerving, hovering between irony and saintly stupidity.

He never saw her become possessed or act as a *banco* or heal anyone. A *banco*'s job is to guide the spirits and protect the person possessed. It was like she was holding off because she had attained some ultimate state of being and become a spirit herself, condensed into a disembodied smile. But later he wondered if something else might have been disturbing her. When he returned to the mountain, years afterwards, the guardians told him she had died and someone else had taken her shed on the flat. She had died of cancer, though quite young.

All his guides died or disappeared like that. Or else like Zaida had been almost killed by the very spirits of the dead with whom they were working and had to give up. It was the mountain that did it. For all its beauty and uplift, you could not forget its danger. He sometimes wondered if the spirit queen would let him finish his book or if anything bad would happen to him. There was no end of people who advised him to stay away. The young woman who had been seduced in her bed at nights by a spirit and had to be taken to a healer to check on her virginity and swore black and blue that people were kidnapped on the mountain and sacrificed in underground caverns. The man in the pastry-shop spreading his arms to make a circle for all to hear how his friend had gone crazy on the mountain and hacked a person into quarters with a machete. The marxist-anarchist actor who presented farces by the sixteenth-century playwright Hans Sachs to the Indians on the Guajria peninsula, but would never ever visit the mountain and relate to the "acting" there because of some inarticulable but massively visceral fear and distaste. The taxi driver from the Canary Islands shaking his head, advising, almost pleading with them to do anything but go there. Repeated warnings not to take the children to the mountain for they would fall sick or be kidnapped by spirits. The obsessive smoking of *tabacos* so as to monitor from the ash the mood of the spirits. The obligatory wearing of the necklaces and armbands of the national colors, together with the Cross of Caravaca, to protect oneself from unmentionable terrors. Then the rock through the car window tearing through Rachel's teeth and mouth at fifty miles an hour that inky night on a country road twenty miles from the mountain. But still he kept coming back. Another friend was raped on the mountain by one of the guardians on a deserted weekday and then she too returned "so as to try to make it all right." In fact she had been petrified from the moment she set foot there, yet from afar, as an idea, shall we say, rather than a reality, the mountain emitted a strange fascination. That was the question.

Katy used to hear voices as she dropped off to sleep when she was sixteen. They were voices of Indians. She told her mother who got frightened and said she was going crazy. The voices continued. Her mother had her examined by doctors and she was locked up in a madhouse, given drugs and shock "therapy." But there a strange thing happened. She was befriended by a woman nurse also who was visited by spirits and used to sneak off and smoke *tabacos* in the washroom. "There's nothing wrong with you!" she said, and threw the medication away. One day the voices told her she was to be free. She packed her bag. Just like that. And from then on she got deeper into the world of the spirits and went to seances in the city.

He wondered how she knew they were voices of Indians and why the images of Indians bore such spirit-force. There were hardly any "real" Indians in the country as a whole, probably less than one percent of the population, and the magical images bore not the slightest resemblance to the "true" Indians but were instead lifted from the fantasy world of the US frontier as the war-bonneted figure of the plains warrior.

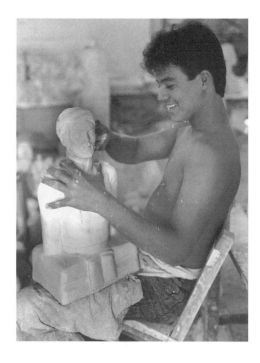

Once he went with Katy to the peak of the mountain known as The Ladder. It was a stiff climb to a rock cliff with a large cave painted inside with the national colors. A ladder led up some fifty feet where, on top of the yellow, blue, and red of the nation's colors, stood not the Liberator, as at the other peak he had visited that day so long ago with Ofelia, but a statue of the spirit queen. Francesco climbed the ladder to pay a promise he'd been meaning to do for two years and while waiting below the stranger asked whether the spirit queen was Indian.

A wiry Black woman emerged from the depths of the cave. She had been gathering candlewax from the offerings by previous pilgrims and had overheard his question. She flatly stated that the spirit queen was Spanish.

Like a hurricane Olympia descended on her livid with rage.

"No! No!," she screamed. "She's an Indian."

She paused. A heaving mountain of a woman catching her breath before the next onslaught.

"Only God knows the history of the spirit queen," she declared, but notwithstanding went on to hold the group enthralled by describing how she, Olympia (obviously of African descent), was actually Indian, pure, unadulterated Indian!

True, she went on, her mother and father were not Indian. But at the moment of her birth, two Indian spirits intervened. Later on in life Olympia had to inform her mother of this and her mother could not stop weeping. Her blood is Indian. It's been proved several times in the US. And while she can receive any blood whatsoever, her own blood is fatal to anyone else. At this very moment, she said, sitting in the shadow of the cave with the national colors sweeping around her, there are four soldiers dying in hospital on account of it.

Later, down in the forest, he came across men possessed by the spirits of Indians. Most wore armbands or headbands of the national colors. They grunted and gesticulated, screaming and threatening. Violence was a big part of it. Sordid and fantastic, bodies twisting with the writhing of possession, flowing through the Arch of Triumph of out-stretched legs to the flag beyond.

A national flag was displayed above their bobbing heads by the *portal,* and he asked a girl aged about twelve why it was there.

"To transform," she replied. "Can't you see that that guy is an Indian, speaking Indian!" And one of the men ran off to pick a plant — any plant it seemed — with which to cure the illness of someone in the crowd, all under the watchful eye and occasionally restraining hand of the woman *banco* mediating between spirits and possessed humans.

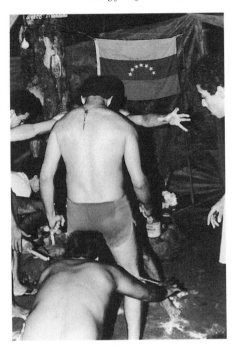

During Easter in 1988 he saw a national flag there the size of a house, some forty feet wide and twenty feet deep. It was suspended between the trees, dwarfing the people.

Another time he saw a man in trance lying in front of a *portal* surrounded by candles. Some twenty-five people stood around watching. He was spreadeagled *under* the national flag!

Spencer, who knows about these things — in so far as they are knowable — said this is done to extract the force of *la patria*.

The U.S. Supreme Court Chief Justice, who also knows about these things — in so far as they are knowable — begins his defense of the flag in Texas versus Johnson (decided June 21, 1989) with the immortal words of Justice Holmes, to wit, "a page of history is worth a volume of logic," and notes that a flag was necessary following independence, for without a flag the British could treat captured seamen as pirates and hang them summarily. It is largely the glory of the flag fluttering over the dead in war that attracts his pen and rouses his ire against its *desecration* (the word tells you all).

But William Burroughs, who also knows of these things in so far as . . . says in *Cities of The Red Night* that the ur-flag, if we may be permitted to coin this concept, the ur-flag of the modern liberal state as founded in the French and American revolutions was that of the eighteenth-century pirate's utopia — now gone forever. "Only a miracle or a disaster could restore it," he says.

Lying spreadeagled under the flag, the miracle stirs, the Chief Justice is being possessed by Captain Mission with his black eye patch.

Nothing could be more deadly, more serious, and more playful, Captain Mission assures him as the Chief Justice screams, his body heaving piteously as if giving birth, expelling the demon within. Knives thunder into the ground around his baby-powdered body laid out in a blazing star of candles. Without the play the spirits would not be attracted. Captain Mission calls on God and holds his knives up to the sky in the form of the Cross. Just the two of them alone up there on the plateau, plus the invisible spirit lodged deep within. You could hear the screams hundreds of yards away.

Lower down the mountain a woman was sunk in an earthen pit with only her curly haired head protruding, the rumpled grey slab of loose soil stretching out like a tomb in front of her chin. A chubby strong man possessed by the Indian Geronimo sprang across her. Then back again. And again.

He had knives in each hand. He would hurtle himself across the body, then crouch down as if copulating with her. He had a strange crawling, stooping, leaping action which would carry him from her head to her feet, grunting and sweating. It was cataclysmically violent and erotic. A woman *banco* hovered in the background.

Further down the mountain the African Bull had possessed a young man of African descent and was holding court. He had metal spikes through his left thigh and talked gutturally in a sort of baby-talk laced with a few English words like "all right," "seven," "woman." His *banco*, a woman in her early thirties, was acting as his interpreter in his consultation with a patient, an elderly woman, while the herbs and medicines recommended were being copied down by the previous patient.

A soldier was among those eagerly waiting in the queue. He was told he'd have to wait a long time. There were many soldiers on the mountain that day. Some of them — maybe all — wanted to be ritually encompassed. After all, so it is said by young men who have completed their military duty, there are Catholic masses in military camps for the spirit queen. They wanted to be purified, to set their body-matter into development. They wanted to be touched and healed by the possessed, yet at the same time with their weapons, their uniforms, and their insignia, they were themselves akin to the spirits and images on the shrines.

At night time spirit-power is stronger. Mission remembered that night in December 1987, walking the line between spirit and matter crossing the river under radiant stars. He and Katy with four of her friends. The danger of the body opening to receive spirit. The camps in the forest lit up in different colors. The Indians at it again. Even crazier than before. Speaking like Indians. Acrobatics. Thumping. Big hands running across big bodies. Running. Screaming. Red. Red for Indians. The old woman *banco* puffing away at her cigar. Walk on! Walk on! said Katy. The spirit queen doesn't like that violence. She'll punish you too.

At times an awesome beauty. Close to midnight they came across four massive bodies under the trees, men and women, great stomachs palpitating, lying like beached whales, face upwards covered with baby powder—natural monuments erupting with painful slowness through the crust of the earth or sinking down into it, each rotund figure a bloated corpse floating on its halo of flames. Watching over them in the darkness of the mountain under the great trees were four equally motionless blank-eyed people. It was an epiphany. No other word for it, Mission thought, as he too sank into the waiting.

The roar of a portable generator pierced the silence. Light bulbs sprang to life swaying overhead in a clearing beyond the trees as another group of pilgrims started to work under plastic sheets. Giant-size Pepsi bottles stood sentry. Further over in another clearing there was a man in a wheelchair with a pathetic saintly face, and another man he guessed was paralyzed lying perfectly flat on his back on two mattresses. On the perimeter of the clearing were plastic buckets, a stove, plates, and spaghetti. The *portal* was simple; candles in the roots of the tree, no flag, no Liberator. On the edge of the darkness stood a young woman in a dressing gown, puffing on a cigar and clicking her fingers. Two men in shorts were lighting candles laid out on a white powdered outline of the human form into which they carried the man from the wheelchair. He couldn't moves his legs and his trembling right arm seemed immobile too. The curer stepped forward, barefoot, a woman with dark hair, an angelic, serious face, dressed in khaki shorts and a blue singlet. They placed a white smock over the sick man. The other woman watched intently, then put the spaghetti on the stove. All Mission could see of the other man were his feet hanging over the edge of the mattresses. He wondered how the woman could call the spirits or concentrate with the noise of the generator from the adjoining camp. She stood at the sick man's feet, puffing furiously on a cigarette, her right hand up in the air as if saluting something. She smoked another cigarette. The waiting was as intense as a knife poised to strike. She put her hand on the man's limbs and her hand seemed weighted with all the hope this universe of ours contains. Then she put her hands on his head.

She kept repeating this. It was so supremely serious, utterly and completely and painfully so, hope hanging on a thread. Her face so true. Her actions so definite. Mission ached watching her working, trying desperately to make this sick man better with his own tensed body.

Next day Katy told him the paralyzed men had not gotten any better. Later he saw them being carried out of the forest across the river and lifted onto the back of a truck.

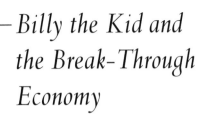

5 — *Billy the Kid and the Break-Through Economy*

Captain Mission is trying to explain to the Chief Justice what goes on here. They are both determined to uphold the honor of the flag. The one for piracy. The other against it. It is an old struggle.

Catharsis, says the Chief.

A thousand plateaus, Mission snaps back, eyes swimming with vibrating intensity.

The Chief insists it's drama but Mission will have none of it as he adroitly throws a knife into the soil by the Chief's right hand. Of course it's dramatic, he snarls. Self-consciously theatrical. How could a spirit otherwise exist? He is contemptuous as he explains to the Chief that it's because of their parlous reality that the spirits of the dead require deliberate artifice as provided by elaborate staging. It's the artifice that allows them to be real he explains. The Chief Justice starts to scream as the spirit within struggles for exit. So much by way of explanation. And then there is the theory of mimetic versatility. Chief screams even louder.

Now it is February 1990, seven o'clock at night at the base of her mountain with twenty pilgrims from the far-off oil-town, the big one by the iridescently blue lake swimming in petrochemistry and putrid remnants of dead fish. The pilgrims stand around, lounging against trees, as if on a movie set, forming a semicircle around a gorgeous *portal* set into a hollowed tree trunk aglow with candlelight. The young man in front of the director of operations otherwise known as the *banco* starts to shake and scream. *Possessed?* Damn straight. But *transported* is the word to use. There's a difference, you know. He's transported by an African. His voice is deep and he keeps shouting *Africa. Viva Africa.* The needles quiver each time he shouts. The needles are about four inches long and go through his cheeks. Ribbons of the national colors are attached to each needle. A drum is being beaten. *Viva Africa.* The ribbons sway. People line up to talk to the spirit.

A young woman with a headband of the national colors starts to shake in front of the *portal*. She smokes a cigar. Could it be the spirit Rosa?

Out of the darkness boldly strides our leader, a big fat man announcing himself as leader of the caravan. He lets it be known he wants respect and he challenges the spirit to announce itself. An untoward visitor, perhaps? Mission adjusts his eyepatch.

The fat man bullies and wheedles. He stoops, he leans forward, he addresses the dark trees and the dark sky beyond. He is the quintessence of all inquisitors and inquisitions that ever were and will be. His body bends with the stress and play of his remorseless questions. A show within a show. And the young woman — or, rather, the spirit transporting her — is no less skillful. They stalk each through the trees. Dueling. Challenging. Disputing.

People sense something is about to happen. They rush to the *portal* to bring him bindings for his arms, bindings for his legs, a white fluffy chest-cover made from rope, and a fabulous feather headdress as big as he is.

In his moment of need he has become transported by an Indian. He looks magnificent and acts magnificent; a fat tall man from the oil town in red bathers and necklace of the national colors, fluffed up and feathered.

Four years later the world news carried a report that one hundred and nine male prisoners had been killed in the highest security prison in that same oil town from which he came. Later reports put the figure above two hundred, but nobody knew the exact number, and it is supposed by many that nobody ever will. Some four hundred Guajiro Indian prisoners had supposedly broken out of their cell-block and fire-bombed the non-Indian prisoners. To all accounts the Indians were beastly. "They mutilated them, butchered them with knives, lynched them, cut their heads off," the pathologist Dr. Bonilla, was reported as saying. "Some of the remains are only fragments."

"It was an act of vengeance," said the prison director, Luís Zambrano. "A Guajiro inmate was decapitated on Thursday by non-Indian prisoners."

But the truth, in so far as what occurs in a prison can ever be ascertained, is not this. Instead of an uprising by Indians what happened was a bloody war between non-Indian prisoners organized in "mafias" in league with the detachment of National Guardsmen who control the prison and profit from the prisoners' needs for food, drugs, alcohol, and firearms . . . this same National Guard that exalts the image of the warring Indian, never to be forgotten hero of the struggle against colonialism whose blood pulses through Olympia's very body.

We can still see that beautiful headdress as he darts his bulk through the trees chasing her hot-footed shadow. Mission watches the line of flight etched by the glowing tip of her cigar through the sultry night air.

She drinks the hot wax from the candles. Her pursuer does too. Someone lights a fire and she jumps into it. The flames are high. She walks on the coals. Later she couldn't remember a thing. She felt no pain. Her feet felt fine.

Mission explains to the Chief that this is a surefire sign of being possessed. He knows his man. This is the sort of legal-sounding thing Chief can engage with. There is a blurred line, you see, between faking and being possessed and, what's more there are degrees of possession; you can be lightly "covered" by a spirit, one-quarter body possessed, one-half, three-quarters, and complete.

There are laws for everything but then there's the inevitable lawlessness created by those very same laws. This is where the action is. The Chief nods. A star witness here is that meticulously careful writer on the sacred in everyday life, a small Frenchman named Leiris. In his study of spirit possession among people in Gondar, Ethiopia, whom he visited in 1933, he concluded some possessions were real, some fake, and most were inbetween. This is a real problem for students of ontology. Even sophisticated anthropologists shy away from its implications for truth and being. Mission warms to his theme. But suddenly the fat man has become a nameless Costaguanian stalking around the glade as a buffoon acting tough spicing his speech with sonofabitch, and faggot, sonofabitch and faggot . . . and the pilgrims get a good laugh out of this.

Ten minutes later yet another spirit arrives, this time a little old lady named Ana from the big oil town. She wriggles into the fat man's body just fine and he shrinks like a prune into a tiny voice speaking English inviting Captain Mission and the Chief Justice to step forward and stop this spectatorial crap and have a little chat. The pilgrims cheer wildly as the Chief, scared witless that his spirit will escape, tries to maintain his dignity as well as his theory of drama. Mission remains cool, calm, and collected. After all, this is his territory. D-territory he insists on calling it. But what's in a name?

Bored with gossip as much as with English, Ana is evacuated by another Costaguanian who — strangely for such a low-life — orders the pilgrims to pair off into the night to make their own plateaus, one person lying down surrounded by burning candles in the inky black-ness, while the other watches. To some people he gave white can-dles. To others, purple ones. The white is for purification, the purple for people afflicted with sorcery. He stuck a fistful into Mission's hand. In the morning he saw they were a deep purple.

Herman Melville wrote a story, "Benito Cereno," about a cargo of African slaves overpowering their masters and, at the approach of another vessel, pretending to be submissive captives once again, commanding the crew to act as if they were still in command and they were still slaves. The story is memorable for the curious atmosphere felt aboard the slave-ship by the sea captain visiting it. Some real. Some fake. Mostly in between.

The jail in the oil town where the massacre had taken place a few months earlier had something of this atmosphere too. There was a fabulation of reality, brought about by the collusion between the more powerful prisoners and their jailers.

By now the human rights groups from the U.S. had been and gone. The Indians from the Guajira had been taken to another prison, and the judge presiding over the massacre had been removed the day before he was to file charges against the National Guard.

The prisoners in this high security prison wore civilian clothes and had the run of the patios most of the day and many of them were visi-bly armed, if only with knives. Rumor had it there were plenty of guns too. The kitchens had no food, the clinic was without medicines, and there was a mere handful of guards (without weapons or uniforms) inside the prison. But outside stood the National Guard.

It was a strange and explosive mix of freedom and imprisonment; an oppressive anarchy of prisoners controlling prisoners through terror and commerce on the inside, and a military cordon outside — a cordon that with money and influence could be broached any time despite its brutal disposition. (In no ways could this be assimilated to the model of the *panopticon* either as fact or metaphor.)

The National Guardsmen looked handsome and fierce posing for a photograph as they adjusted their bullet-proof vests, red berets, and gleaming weaponry at the foot of the life-sized Christ hanging on the cross at the entrance to the jail. A force to contend with.

Yet Aguito, the head of one of the two gangs of prisoners involved in the massacre, used to slip out of jail at night to attend to business, and return in the morning.

The question is: Why did he bother to return?

One day the judge was surprised to get a telephone call from Aguito asking advice on selling some paintings of Picasso he had gotten, stolen from a gallery in Texas two months earlier.

In the week Captain Mission spent there one prisoner "escaped" — if that's the appropriate word to use for such a situation — and another was stabbed to death. That was about average. Once there was rumor of a disturbance and the National Guard came jogging in a long line into the prison, rusty machetes swinging.

The prisoners were "free" inside the prison: free to buy and sell the necessities of life as well as drugs and weapons sold to them by the National Guard or with their permission, and without this freedom they could not live because otherwise the prison provided vitually nothing by way of basic necessities. The prison illustrated to perfection the same confluence of force and fraud constituting the state of the whole and its fantastic creation of the entity known as the national economy.

Without the cordon of force — and fraud — this break-through economy would not function. Official, and Extra-Official. You can never have one without the other. The point here is neither descriptive nor moralistic concerning corruption. The point here is the need to uphold law so that corruption can occur. In such a situation — global in extent, although varying in intensity as between Nation-States — the break-through economy of taboo and transgression generates wealth and satisfaction of desire through transgressing interdiction. We are a long way from models of supply and demand which, from the point of view of break-through economics, look pathetically simple-minded. Adam Smith's invisible hand is as nothing as compared with the magic of the state and the public secret of the official and the extra-official wherein lurk the spirits of the dead that a history bequeaths the state of the whole.

There was a small bust of the Liberator in the front patio of the prison. It stood disproportionately small on a tall column. (A pin-headed Liberator?) There was a bullet hole through his back as if no one had had the guts even during the massacre to shoot him face to face, properly deface him, that is.

On the front wall of the prison, facing the street, facing *freedom* — if that's the appropriate word — was painted a triptych. To one side was the flag and the national coat-of-arms. In the center was a portrait of the Liberator. And on the other side was this slogan, as if spoken by the Liberator:

You are part of my heart
For liberty
For justice
For the great and the beautiful

A people who love independence
Will eventually succeed.

And male prisoners hung through the bars on the second floor making love in sign language to the women prisoners several hundreds of yards away.

Meanwhile, four blocks from the church half an hour's drive from the prison, one of the choir boys named Jesus took Mission late Friday night to a cinder-block house at the bottom of a steep gully in a lower-middle-class *barrio*. Out back there was a little shed with black plastic sheeting for a roof, flapping in the wind. There was a notice painted on the mud wall giving the price for a consultation. It was dark and Mission was asked if he was wearing a black or a blue shirt. It seemed like a strange question. "Blue!" he replied. From the shed came a scrunched up, high-pitched, voice.

A woman in her forties with dyed blonde hair and the face of a battered angel-mother, together with a flabby-faced young man speaking excellent English, put him at his ease. They smiled as if in possession of a grand secret. Mission was told to take off his shoes and enter the shed—properly called a *centro*.

All of one wall was taken up by a huge *portal* or shrine. To the left there was a three-foot-high statue of *El Indio* Guaicaipuro. On the right was a similarly large statue of *El Negro* Primero, while in the center was a massive statue of the spirit queen. On the extreme right was a bronze-colored statue of the Liberator, about a foot in height. Densely occupying all remaining space were scores of candles, portraits, and figurines of spirits. It was dark but for the candles and the dim light of a naked bulb draped with red cloth. At the center of attention for the several people therein was this tremulous high-pitched voice coming from nowhere and extending everywhere.

It was a hefty fellow under a crumpled cowboy hat talking—if that's the word—with a white haired old lady. He greeted Mission cordially, pulled his hat further down, and invited questions about the spirit world, his answers, to Mission's irritation, being meticulously translated into English by the flabby-faced young man. The answers, no less than the questions, seemed *pro forma* and irrelevant.

Abruptly and without ceremony the spirit bade farewell, grabbed Mission's hand and blessed him with the sign of the cross, evacuating the body just in time for the arrival of the spirit of the Indian Kinka. He took off his shirt and sat cross-legged on the ground with a feather in his hair. He couldn't speak Spanish, it seemed, and grunted petulantly, pent up with fury.

"He's real angry!" someone whispered in fear.

He splashed rum over his body and glowered. In the dark by the *portal* softly lit with its myriad images his face started to stretch and fill out until it resembled the heavy features of the *caciques* sold as plaster busts in the stores of magic or those faces on the gold coins designed by Vallenilla for the dictator in the 1950s.

It was an amazing transformation.

Young men with headbands of the national colors came out of the dark to stand over and shield him.

There was a girl there aged about nine and the Indian lifted her up by the waist until she was face to face with the statue of the spirit queen. She began to tremble.

Battered Mother Angel-Face nudged Mission knowingly. "When the girl is thirteen a spirit will descend into her." Mission smiled.

The spirit let the little girl down but she stayed mesmerized in front of the spirit queen for another ten minutes as the Indian began to converse with Mission, bemoaning the fate of Indians whom the Spaniards had hunted down with dogs.

"Goodbye," he said without warning, blessing Mission with a firm handshake, and then Billy arrived — Billy, from the Criminal Court, *La Corte Malandra.*

He had on a small trilby hat, a can of beer in one hand, a cigarette in the other. His stomach stuck out aggressively and in between sucking on his cigarette and his beer he would utter with immense satisfaction, while slapping the other young men on the shoulders, "Focky Fock! Focky Fock!"

Everyone laughed. His was a sad story.

Abandoned by his mother in the capital on a garbage heap while still a baby, he was saved by a poor Black woman who raised him together with her many other children. As Billy grew, he saw his new brothers and sisters starving. There was no way to make money other than by crime, so he stole from the rich to give to the poor. His voice died away in the dark.

Mother Angel-Face repeated the last line. "I stole from the rich to give to the poor." The little girl had stopped trembling. It was close to midnight.

An ear-splitting roar filled the valley followed by the scream of a police siren. A raid. Motorbikes circling in a frenzy of sirens and racing engines. The motor cut and in walked — if such a banal term can be used for the entry of a god — the most immaculate, uniform-pressed, handsome young police officer who ever sat astride a motorbike.

He was late for the seance but welcome nevertheless.

Outside Mission admired the policeman's motorbike, also immaculate, huge and sleek, white and chromed, with a flashing blue light. "Same as in Los Angeles," the policeman said.

Mission asked Mother Angel-Face, she with the battered face, what he owed. "Nothing," she said. He had contributed a large bottle of rum. As he turned to go he was asked to greet a tubby young man in white shorts with a dirty bottom, shy, awkward, and beefy, about twenty-seven years old. Mission offered his hand and stepped back in surprise.

It was the *materia*! The spirit medium. The body possessed by the spirits! The transition was more than startling. It gave cause for wonder. Just a plain young man all awkward and insignificant staring at the ground — he who had been taken by the dead, by old cowboys from the *llanos*, by Indians from the high Andes stomping through the centuries of pain and mayhem, by criminals from the slums of the capital, he who possessed by the Indian had held young girls up high trembling face to face with the queen herself — now shrouded in this other sort of grace that comes with shyness.

Next day Mission took some clothes around to the woman who washed for the Catholic priest. The door opened. There stood the beautiful lady with the face of a battered angel. It was she who washed the priest's clothes. The previous night was already washed away.

You are part of my heart
For liberty
For justice
For the great and the beautiful

A people who love independence
Will eventually succeed.

6 — *Holy Torpor*

On the eve of the Liberator's birthday, 24th of July, 1990, Virgilio took Mission to a different part of the mountain. This was Quiballo, and Katy's lip curled in disgust for it was ugly and contemptible, the part of the mountain to which people went to do bad things, she said. Huge crowds would come for the Liberator's birthday, he was told, but by the time he and Virgilio arrived at eight that night, only one car was there, the place was gloomy beyond words, and Mission's despair reached bursting point, as though Quiballo gave license to vent his troubled feelings about the mountain as a whole.

For despite what Katy and so many others had told him, it wasn't that Quiballo was all that different, dismal and evil, as against the rest of the mountain's zest and goodness. It wasn't as if there were two separate and homogenous parts, one positive, the other negative. Rather, in their own ways, both Quiballo and the rest of the mountain were mixtures of these things and it was the mixing itself that was the power the mountain emitted. The problem was that ambiguity to this degree resisted logic and stasis while demanding both. It was impossible to contain and ritual was designed precisely to tap into that impossibility while, on the other hand, were these mawkish attempts by the conscious mind to unravel the impossible ambiguities by territorializing them so as to grant clear substance — the evil of Quiballo, for instance, as contrasted with the uplift of the other sites, such as Sorte where he had first gone with Ofelia many years before. But wasn't he, in retrospect, repeating this same maneuver on himself by manipulating his memories, hugging to his chest the beauty and transcendent grace of that day on the mountain with Ofelia, a memory made all the more precious by her disappearance since then and his hope their paths would one day cross?

Katy's daughter had brought Mission here once before. Walking on the far side of the river they had come across a sheet of newspaper with the cross of Caravaca burnt onto it by gunpowder. It was magic to kill a child, she commented off-handedly.

Mission remembered hordes of people there that first time in Quiballo, stomachs roped in by national colors and red bathing costumes, red of warring and of the Indian, clustered by their shrines becoming possessed some screaming others in trance, people flipping out, people flipping in, get the enemy, become purified, the sacred billowing forth in waves of ecstasy and decay through vacant-eyed stares in mud under imperiled skies, stench of sodden refuse wet newspaper plastic bags juice cartons red plastic containers of gunpowder soda cans cigarette wrappers talcum powder rotting fruit and food heaped high on the shrines vaporizing in tropical heat. Roots running like knotted varicose veins along the earth, trees dripping overhead.

The next time Virgilio refused to take him to Quiballo. It was getting dark, he said, shaking his head. Nothing would move him. It's too dangerous, he said. A priest was held up there recently and robbed of all he had. Virgilio knew the amount stolen, to the cent.

So Mission found a seat in a jeep stuffed with twelve people and a kid on the roof soaked in the rain. They got there around seven thirty at night, drums beating, flames in the distance casting leaping shadows on clusters of figurines and shrines, slippery underfoot, ink-black sky overhead, the smell of old sweat as he walked past the shacks protected by an eight foot high steel fence erected by some branch of government set on concrete blocks and topped by strands of barbed wire. For Quiballo not only had a reputation for evil spirits. It was also where the park rangers had their office and living quarters.

Everything looked and smelled as though poised just this side of the apocalypse; the shit-stirred mud, the stale sweat, the decay, the just-sitting, the color tv with crowds jumping up and down in front of a rock band, everyone watching silent and motionless.

The apocalypse on hold.

No catastrophic outburst. No creative destruction. No vomiting out of inward turned violence. Just an intensifying surging decay where life and death merged in a turbulent morass of ever-heaving forms. "Would the object nauseate if it offered nothing desirable?"

Towards the river the drumming became stronger, accompanied by a rhythmic shouting. "Force." "Force" . . . Or was it the sound of the river? He passed car after car in the parking lot. The driver of the jeep had said fifteen thousand people come out here on a weekend. More like two thousand, or less. Points of light along the river became clearer. Serpentine paths led by pools of mud and plastic camps reflecting the candlelight wandering over the screaming body of a man being possessed, standing over the body of a woman lying in trance, her body covered with herbs and spongy cattle lungs and liquor. In a hollow in a tree trunk was a beautiful shrine centered on statues of the Three Potencies with the *India* Mara beneath a bronze colored bust of the Liberator illuminated feebly by a stout candle of the national colors. It was a group of people from the border state of Apure. Mission spoke with one, a welder, who explained that they were preparing both *materia* and *alma*, body and soul, but that the man screaming had encountered obstacles. At that moment the screaming man began to shake and go into trance.

All around were other groups in different stages of possession. Mission wandered from group to group, stumbling like a drunk, infatuated, senses reeling.

Down by the river it was calm, the eye of the storm. Next to the footbridge across the river some thirty people were inhaling cigars, squatting in front of a large tiled shrine about fifteen feet wide that looked as though it had been built many years ago, perhaps in the 1950s. Now and again a person would hawk phlegm and spit tobacco juice, breaking the silence. Here one asked permission from the spirit queen before crossing the river into the mountain proper. It was the one shrine at which just about everyone stopped before entering the mountain. Nobody went into more than a light trance.

Bursting out of the tiled wall shoulder to shoulder at the center of the shrine were the Three Potencies. They were bursting forth from the national flag.

To their right, suitably reserved and aloft on a small hillock of blue cement, hand on sword, stood the Liberator.

Next to this amazing *portal* there was a little wooden house, more like an oversized doll's house, painted pink, raised three feet with a fragile verandah. The front wall was glass and padlocked and Mission had to cup his hands to his face to see anything. Even though there was a lantern flickering a red light, it was dark inside. But he could distinguish a life-sized statue of the spirit queen dressed in lace and veils with huge roses and a gold chain ("a gift from La Guyanía," he was told, referring to a *misión* from the far-off state of the name). All around her lay gifts, or rather promises paid to her; money, and many, but many, wedding dresses hung together along one side.

José's son told him they were the dresses of actual brides.

Obscured by the dresses was a painting of an army officer. There seemed several more such paintings behind the dresses. By means of such portraits, officers in the armed services pay a promise. To one side hung a portrait of the Liberator.

Of all the things Mission had seen on the mountain this fragile little house struck him as the strangest, this reliquary of miracles repaid by portraits of soldiers and the flowing laces of brides stuffed together with the Liberator.

By the first *portal* someone had painted a map of the spiritual geography of the mountain as could be followed from Quiballo. From this Mission could see it was as much a magic river as a magic mountain, for the line of spirit-force followed the river bed as depicted by the chain of innumerable shrines on the map, the majority of them, he guessed, forming pools in the river bed, with names of the spirits to be invoked in each locale —*don Juan de las potencias, India hechicera* Jenoveba (spelled *hechisera*), Makumba, Juan del Chaparro, Gran Chacao, Mister burburo and Cha[n]go de Nigeria, Indiana, Cacique Coromoto, Tamara Castillo, Cacique Mara, Cacique Sorocaima, Cacique Atahualpa, Juan el borracho, don Juan de la calle, Negro Pio . . . and many more.

The national flag had a prominent place two thirds of the way up, alongside big letters announcing *the Fortress of the Liberator*, after which the line of spiritual power veered off at a tangent to ascend to the three houses of each of the Three Potencies, side by side with the cave of the *Negra* Dorotea.

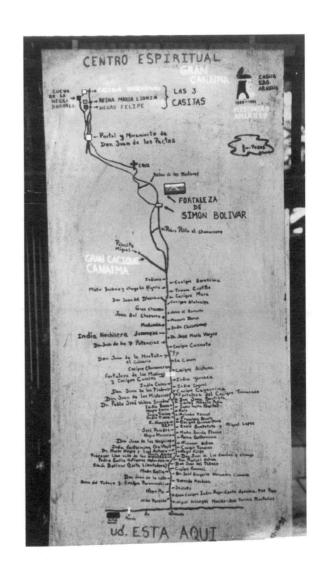

Embossed in metal hung a sign near the map:

> **The domain of the Spirit Queen is sacred. Respect and don't profane it with envy and evil. This site is a sanctuary where only good can be practised. Those who try to do evil will be punished. This is the law of the queen: love, solidarity, understanding.**
>
> *In the mountain, 31 of January 1976,*
> *Edmundo Rosal*

And close by was posted an official-looking green notice with stark white lettering from the government's park service listing a large number of things prohibited — including Mission noted, *sacrifice* and taking *photographs*.

A barefoot leprechaun of a man named Bolívar, in ragged clothes stiffened and yellowed in sweat, took Mission to *the Fortress of the Liberator*. It was raining. The ascent was steep and slippery. The stream was roaring.

The higher you go, the more spiritual it gets, Bolívar said, noting that down there at the entry to the mountain the power is practically exhausted. It was a scary concept, this continuous excavation of the base forcing one ever higher.

After half an hour of climbing they crossed the stream and came to a cave in a rock face. The interior was painted in the stripes of the national colors, now somewhat faded. Giant trees formed a backdrop, leaves glistening in the downpour. Seven young people were crouched around a glass-covered portrait of the Liberator suspended over a small shrine together with two national flags, a small one jutting out of the rock and a large, semi-furled one, by the side of the shrine. The slippery space was so narrow that the people resembled a chain of mountain climbers clinging one to the other with barely room to move — saints and spirits poised on the edge of nothingness.

Bolívar squatted to one side, thankful to be out of the cold rain, and lit up a *tabaco* he'd found by the shrine.

People were becoming possessed in turns. A young man in wet red shorts was on his back, shoulders heaving, stomach thrown forwards, herbs and medicines over his bare chest, honey in the form of the cross on his forehead, inner elbows, and knees, so as to make him less violent. He trembled for what seemed like half an hour then got up and almost fell off the cliff as another man took his place.

It was the mixture of routine and sensationalism that Mission found disturbing.

As the next man lay down, someone fished out a bunch of needles wound together with thin red, blue and yellow ribbons. People drew hard on their *tabacos* to concentrate the power as rum and Cinzano were poured over his now inert figure. After a short spell of quivering the man uttered a high pitched cry so startling it was like his entire being had become ejected into voice. He was given a red robe with a gold border for he had become possessed by Santa Barbara and his companions set to work impaling his cheeks and thighs with the needles. Thus embodied and pinioned, blood streaming with the national colors, Santa Barbara proffered blessings and advice there in the cave cut into the rainswept mountain. Time stood still, like sludge. People moved their limbs like lead with infinite slowness and great deliberation, eyes staring. Even Bolívar stepped forward and entered into the strange cross-arm "embrace" with the saint which initiates the blessing. He was told with much solemnity that he had an enemy, but that he would, nevertheless, find work.

Santa Barbara was the possessed man's patron saint. He always works with her and knows he's going to get possessed by her. You can tell, said Bolívar told Mission, because when he gets possessed, he *really* gets possessed. Not three quarters, not half, or half a half, but the full thing! That's why he can go on for so long.

And on he went, national colors drooping a little while the young woman guiding these young men lay on her back, half asleep in the black mud just this side of the pelting rain. They had been there three days already.

Bolívar explained that half or more of such spirit leaders are women — "because they have more soul than men." And when the leaders are men, they are often homosexual — which means the risk of being arrested and sent to a concentration camp, Bolívar said, in his melodramatic way, near Puerto Boyacá in the jungle, and thereafter having to carry an identification card from the Department of Health indicating one is not carrying a venereal disease or HIV. It's a way of getting out of the army, Bolívar added, but then you'll never get a job anywhere.

He was very nervous: about the rising stream, about the spirits, about everything. If the National Guard find you using the flag or the image of the Liberator like this, watch out! he warned.

It was cold as they clambered down in the late afternoon over roots and boulders by the torrential stream, minds numb, faces lashed by rain.

Later in his notes Mission wrote of the torpor paralyzing him. Like the possessed, was he too condemned never to remember?

Worse still, he couldn't care less.

It was as if he had been reduced to the same glassy-eyed routine of the exotic as the people in the cave. In the end it was apathy that stole the show. The skyrockets illuminated the heavens with their fiery stars only to have the darkness close in firmer than before. It was not just Mission, the voyeur. That was the worst of it. It was everyone. It was everything. The soul shrank like a snail at the touch of the divine into the most inaccessible parts of being, leaving calcified layers of abjection like hardened flesh. What little energy Mission could muster was channeled into frustration turning on itself because of his inability to convey, as he put it in his notes, "just how incredibly weird it was last night out at Quiballo — close to the same league as the very first night at Sorte" (where he had gone for the first time to the mountain with Ofelia, in 1983).

When he re-read this he didn't at first see the qualification of the reference. It was not the first trip to Sorte with Ofelia, but the first *night* of that trip. Taken as a whole that trip had been full of beauty and wonder.

But the night preceding the ascent, that was something else. And while in retrospect the night was necessary to the day that followed, the crucial thing was that that day did follow and that after a hard day's work the gunpowder crackled and shook on top at the Liberator's palace, Dante did find his Beatrice or, rather, Haydée, after the dark confusion of the woods, did find her Liberator — *whereas* in Quiballo in its entire complicated totality it was as if there was no point beyond the guardians' shack.

In other words the mountain fanning out from the gloom of Quiballo was the insides of the guardians' shack, magnified. The narrative had gotten stuck in atmosphere, vaporous intimation as thick as the clotted nothingness of the wet night outside and the hammer blows of spirit-kitsch of the shrines inside — like the aimless whorls traced by the guardians milling around their earth-floored shed at Sorte at the base of the mountain that night many a year ago. It was the spirit they collectively generated, muttering dire warnings about the danger of the mountain, eyebrows raised, glazed expressions, warnings coated in candle grease and cigar smoke clinging to the lace brocade of the queen's many dresses, the rancid air all the heavier on account of the concentration that the mountain allows the spirits, milling around, moving invisibly, searching for a body.

Hadn't Virgilio explained to him nursing his taxi over the back country roads that this nation was full, just full, of spirits lurking in pools of water and obscure drains, desperate for a nice warm body to take over? It is these the spirit-mediums invoke when they wish to do harm. Hadn't Virgilio's estranged wife, Zaida, once a mighty spirit healer herself, ably assisted by her beautiful daughters, also told him that spirits are everywhere looking for a body? But other not so innocent spirits are looking too. It was one of these that took her by the throat and would have slowly killed her had it not been for the pure absoluteness with which she abandoned the mountain and entered the temple of the Evangelists, now singing her throat out each and every day and sometimes twice a day. For this is the danger; the very opening of the *materia* to the entry of spirit is fraught with the demon.

All the more wonderful, then, the great theater on the mountain performed along that tightrope — those bellicose Indians, those English speaking Africans, those vulgar Costaguanians, and the sweet old lady from the oil town, not to mention other cross-dressing and the beautiful *Negra* Francesca.

The mountain always had this potential to metamorphose the gloom and the fear into carnivalesque.

But that was not its genius. That was easy. Dialectics. Reversals. Co-dependencies. Two sides of the old coin we now know so well. You don't need no spirit queen nor the magic of the state to flip it over.

Virgilio drove slowly back to town. They gave a lift to a woman who said she'd been cured recently. The *ánima sola* had possessed her and she was lucky to be still in the land of the living.

Mission took the opportunity to have a professional conversation with José regarding his views on the *velación*, the body on the ground face up in front of a *portal*, going into trance in a circle of flame. How did it work? Why do you do it? Mission was still intrigued and naive enough to think there were clear answers and that José, with the innocence of youth, might know. An old trick. Mission was adept. But so was José who began not with the living, but with the dead. Not with bodies, but with spirits, for most of whom he had little time as they are of *bajo luz* — low level luminosity — as compared, say, with the Libertator and his court who are of *alto luz*. The low-light types hunger for light and are anxious to progress and hence can be bought through prayers and the Catholic mass to invade the body of one's enemy.

Spirits of *bajo luz* are stupid, like dogs, and easily bought with the promise of a body. This creates problems.

What a spirit economy, marveled Mission. One advanced in light towards the Liberator by selling oneself as an assassin! Or, if not exactly an assassin, as a take-over expert slipping into the body of the other! What a sick world we live in. The sickness of power. The mad judge Daniel Paul Schreber's world of bodies gobbling other bodies, swelling with power, fighting for warmth in range wars coursing through stellae. Or the professor on the top floor, his body enlarging by the minute by the side of his skulls and computer print-outs as he plans to swallow the whole fourth floor faculty for compost for the roof garden lab dedicated to saving, or at least studying, what's left of the world's flora and fauna. What do they know about science, he snarls self-reflexively, but his words are already lost in a vile attack of hermeneusis as he realizes with a sickening shudder that his adaptive potential to postmodernity is just about all used up.

"Now, in a *velación*," went on José, "a person goes into trance and the possessing spirit is forced to talk out of the mouth of the entranced. "I gave her this headache." "I gave him that pain in the stomach." And so on. Then it's the curer's job to extract the spirit. The spirit may even confess who put it into the body. Sometimes the curer needs to ask other spirits for assistance." Mission remembered what Virgilio had told him earlier about the country swarming with spirits of low light under every rock in every drain and puddle aching for a body, ready to do anything for purification. It was an original and dynamic view of the modern Nation-State that Mission could appreciate. Not that there weren't some genuine intellectual issues here; for instance how could the search for purification involve such impure methodologies and why did there have to be so much sheer schlock? Not that Mission minded. Transgression was his game. And the only frontier left to be crossed was that of taste, he assured the Chief, as his mind flicked back to the scenes by the river where the Indian stalks the thundering ground in the muggy night spongy underfoot by the human body floating in talcum powder, white candles at the joints, the one at the groin a hieroglyph readied to explode into the future.

And this was not restricted to Quiballo. No way. He remembered stories Katy had told him at Sorte, like when the National Guard, with whom she was on the best of terms, told her of their recent shoot-out with *guerrilla* fighters at another entrance to the mountain, surely a total fantasy, and how, she went on, through some bizarre train of associations, a foreign man and woman had just been mugged, the

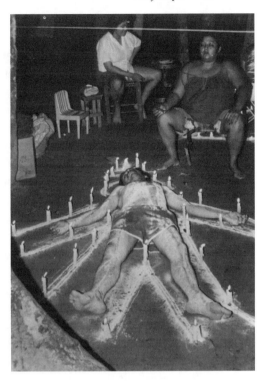

man killed and the woman raped, prone on the murdered man's back. No wonder her daughter never entered the mountain without a machete concealed in her clothing. Mission remembered the balding, muscley, middle-aged man telling him in a bakery in the capital how his friend had been possessed at the mountain and in front of his very own eyes had cut a woman into pieces. First he cut off her head. Then he split her trunk in two. He'd been driven to it, said the bald man, by the *demonio*, and he warned against ever setting foot there. He himself had immediately abandoned the whole thing and become a Jehovah's Witness. His eyes shot fire as he told the story, there, anonymous, next to the chrome and glass counters holding the newly baked bread and pastries.

It is a lonely week day and Mission feels sad, so he sets out to visit Zambrano. He is anxious but doesn't know why. It is starting to get to him. He hesitates to get out of the taxi and be left alone. The driver looks at him strange. He wears a cowboy hat and is an ardent believer in the spirit queen. He waits patiently for Mission to make up his mind. Finally Mission gets out and slowly crosses the river into the woods alone where a friend of his had been violated by the guardians years before. A centipede creeps along an abandoned *portal*. A spirit from the anti-colonial wars? Never have the trees seemed taller, the earth more desolate. A crazy man in leaky shoes comes splattering along the riverbed muttering about being mugged by two guys with shotguns. With relief Mission returns across the river to meet up with Zambrano.

It's been eight years since they last talked, each lost in their own mission, and now Zambrano was so thoroughly at home in his mysticism that he was completely rational even though he called himself a *brujo*, which in English translates as *witch*. But English has its own history in these matters. He himself, he said with emphasis, never became possessed by spirits. Oh, no! He seemed overly preoccupied with realness, assuring the stranger that ninety-five percent of all spirit possessions there were fake. And on top of that there was *mucho invento*, like the *Vikingos* such as Eric the Red. He sat and contemplated the beyond in his brown-checked Bermuda shorts, wiping at the sweat, his dogma sustained by a constant high from nicotine and Pepsi soaking through rolls of fat on his stomach.

Most of the people who come to him for cure are suffering, he said, from psychosomatic illnesses. Few are afflicted with an invading spirit. As an example of the latter he cited the case of the wife of a captain of the National Guard. She was possessed by the spirit of a dead man who was in love with her and, invisible as he was, would copulate with her in front of the captain! The captain was amazed. His own wife fucking herself, so it appeared, on being fucked by the spirit within her! *Contorsiones extrañas*, was how Zambrano put it in his clinical manner. He needed four strong men from the National Guard to hold her down when he exorcised the spirit by the river. Her face became monstrous as the struggle developed and at one point she lifted straight off the ground. Zambrano's eyebrows quivered along with the fatty folds on the underside of his upraised arms. It was very quiet.

Stories of extremity were legion and so much part of the mountain that you could only conclude they were extensions of its sacred power —the verbal equivalent of *portales* brought to life by spirit possession, magical gateways spread over the mountain's surface, wounds open to the sky overflowing with the aura of the dead concentrated in the court of the spirit queen.

What a resource!

Like oil, the amount and production of which was a closely guarded state secret.

Only instead of being used for petrodollars to swell the purse of state, this treasure of self-renewing living death could possess, through wild expenditure, an entire Nation-State. And who, mused Mission, could exorcise that?

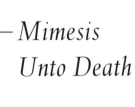

7 — *Mimesis Unto Death*

Theaters of spirit possession on the magic mountain might, then, be thought of as like the stories of the storyteller, theatricalised stories that specialize in rehearsals summoning death to the stage of the living human body so as to render, through repeat performance, the authority of death that lies at the source of the story-form.

What happens, however, is not much more than an obsession with the rehearsal itself, as if by such means an abstracted authority or meta-authority could be siphoned off—and it is precisely this abstracted authority, with its debt to both death and the storyteller put into question by modernity, which seeps as formal rationality into the fundament of modern law and bureaucracy, very much including the modern state.

Here with this notion of a surplus of death-authority, transforming into the abstraction of the thing-in-itself garnered through continuous rehearsal, we come to the image of the human animal miming death as a form of defense, an image at the basis of Nietzsche's awesome critique of power in the West and developed by Horkheimer and

Adorno with their notion of *the organization of mimesis* — a primitivist appropriation of the mimetic faculty crucial to the instituting of power as rationality in modern bureaucratic organization of which the exemplar is the state. In this regard they highlight the importance of a *mimesis unto death* in which the subjective spirit "can master a despiritualised nature only by imitating its rigidity and despiritualising itself in turn."

This mimesis unto death as the life-force of administrative and legal reason opens our eyes to a whole new way of thinking death and the state — of the possibility for a history of the mimesis of death-forms fatefully involved in the social intelligence of modern corporate organization and deception, no less than in the functioning of state-forms and their associated epistemologies of the subject as subject of stately being. Thus the *cogito ergo sum*, for all its importance for the new self of modernity, yields to *"I die, therefore I am"* and once again the spotlight reverts, through modernity's primitivism, to the labor of the negative.

How fitting, therefore, how laden with possibilities for stately representation, is spirit possession — especially under the mantle of influence of the spirit queen. For here not only is mimesis unto death the political art-form par excellence, repeated and worked over continuously, and not only is this obsession itself obsessively at the service of the embellishment of the space of death created as memorial to the founding violence, but in addition death is inflected through the shadowy female consort of the legitimating figure of the Liberator so as to fortify the "break-through economy" of taboo and transgression in which the authority imparted by the looks of the dying is harvested first in the entranced body lying perfectly still in its halo of flame, and then in frenzied body-contorting, eye-staring, performance.

The first mode, that of stillness, is the *velación*, in which the body mimics death as corpse — a beatified and beautified corpse metamorphosing, so doctrine has it, into pure matter and thus readied for the second mode.

The second mode is that of the corpse-body brought "alive" by the incorporation of the possessing spirit. Here image and body interpenetrate in what we might call the "theater of physiognomies." Spirit possession on the magic mountain, like film and photography, magnifies physiognomy — the obscure but confident commonplace practice of interpreting insides from outsides, human character and disposition from the face — only in the case of spirit possession there is a sort of physiognomic reversal. Here the inside presumes or is presumed to exert its physiognomic magnification onto the outside, spirit is writ large onto the moving screen that is the body now housing it.

The staging of the spirit queen's mountain is thus an interconnected dual stage, the staging of the corpse and the staging of physiognomies. And if it is principally because of the mimesis unto death, as the life of stately being, that the strange corporeal rigidities of spirit possession find an appropriate staging (first mode), then it is the play with history writ into the mobile mass of the body that awaits the touch of spirit in the theater of physiognomies (second mode).

The first mode ordains and predetermines the second as the flip side of the tumescent force of taboo that gives to the corpse its splendor. This flip side to mimesis unto death is the *state of emergency* where a completely different form of stately mimesis is unleashed.

Now the corpse springs to life. Intense action takes command in which the exception is the rule, entailing simulation, dissimulation, speed, sudden changes of pace and, above all, the presence of the sovereign spiritualised as he who decides on the exception. Nevertheless he could not do this, nor the exception obtain as rule, without death-work under the supervision of the spirit queen.

Death-work, as Walter Benjamin suggested, provides the authority required by the storyteller, and such work entails the sudden revelation of a sequence of images of the self set in motion, so he thought, *inside* a dying person as life approached its end.

But could not this *memoire involontaire* triggered by bodily sensation and bodily circumstance, in this particularly poignant case by life's end, be *externalised* in a theatricalised version of itself, as in spirit possession?

Here we should be mindful of the fact that for most people for most of world history, spirit possession was the norm. Whatever feeble capacity the West itself had to mobilize death this way, modernity erased with a vengeance. We can but speculate what riches would have been available to Benjamin's storyteller had this mode been theatricalized and its at times open, at times hidden dependence on death-work been made more recursive. All we have now is the death of death . . .

Such theatrics requires a stage in space and time — as in the case of this ex-colony with its death-space built from stately poetics of anti-colonial warring fused to apocalyptic triumphalism. The spirit queen's mountain is the supreme attempt to stage and restage just this moving space.

In looking forwards to the past, death-revelation creates an uncanny time-space dimension and does so in tandem with a surging revelation as to self-consciousness. This is what's at stake in the paradox with which Benjamin suggests that the image-sequence revealed to the dying person is "views of himself under which he encountered himself without being aware of it" — death providing through this strange pictorial turnabout a prime instance of what Benjamin saw as central to his method of the *dialectical image*.

It's as if death reveals an irreducible alterity in the self, namely the social *persona*, a word also meaning mask, for death has the license to bring forth the mask at the curtain call on life, it being the social role of death to illuminate role-playing itself, and this applies with singular force to meta-death, the formative experience of modernity which makes it possible to see a new beauty in what is vanishing with the death of death.

8 — *Spiritual Treachery*

"After she left," said Zaida, "I used to feel the cold of the spirits passing behind me. The girl had gone but her spirits hung around.

"I was outside grinding corn. I smelt cigar smoke. My kids were lighting up those cigars the girl had left. I liked the smell and then I felt myself rising in a rush of coldness. I saw lights in a drain.

"My soul had left and Lino Valle's spirit had entered me!"

Her daughter, interrupted. "I was there," she said. "I felt her body. It was cold. Her spirit had left and was replaced by a spirit from that drain, a woman from Valencia!"

"Next time it happened, four spirits came: Lino Valle, the queen María Lionza, the queen Margarita, and don Martín Canete. When you're in that state you can heal people, you help them get money, and you can help them in their love life," she explained.

Yes! Even the spirit queen possessed her. And did so many times.

What's more, she'd been possessed by her own mother-in-law!

Who then proceeded to scold her! Can you

believe it! There she was possessed by her mother-in-law who had the nerve to berate her!

"You feel a force, a strong force," she replied when he asked how it felt to be possessed. "You feel it throughout the body, most of all in the arms as if someone was tying you up. A force external to yourself. Your back and shoulders swell up as if someone was putting air into them and then you feel nothing until you come back to normal. Then you feel tired and sore for about three days, especially the muscles of the shoulders.

"*El Negro* Felipe, he was the one who came most often. He would say he needed rum and everyone should drink rum. He would drink up to seven bottles! And he was vulgar. He would tell women they were looking for men.

"So many spirits arrived that I can't really remember. But I'll tell you one thing. Spirits are no good for anybody! You're always their instrument!

"There was María Lionza. She would wear a cape and a crown. And then there was a demon, disguised as María Lionza. That's the spirit that caused the illness."

Her daughter Nieves broke in again. "I used to cry all the time. It was not my mother any more."

Zaida laughed.

It was a curious conversation, this probing by Mission into spiritual history, because the possessions were beyond memory or, to be precise, were split between two irreconcilable zones, one of which was generally beyond recall. The subject split then evaporated, so to speak. Once a woman came up to Zaida and said you're the person who cured me! But Zaida didn't remember her at all. Her daughter said Yes! She had treated her. But Zaida had been possessed and had no recollection.

The first person she cured after Lino Valle's spirit entered her was a little girl aged one and one-half years whom no doctor could cure. She had measles and was suffering from diarrhea and vomiting and Zaida cured her in the house using plants. She was not possessed although she invoked the Three Potencies, smoked cigars, and recited The Lord's Prayer. The child started to improve that night and was normal in three days.

"Once in the early morning," she continued," I saw in a dream a car coming from the capital with many people. There were two kids vomiting blood, a boy and a girl. In the dream I prepared a *velación* with lots of grapes and apples and plants. . . . That very same day they came to my house! From the capital! We went out to the mountain — to the same place that I had seen in the dream near Sorte — and I recreated the same *velación* that I had seen in the dream. The *portal* too. The same."

She didn't use portraits or statues, but she did use candles — red, blue, yellow, and white. "These are the rays that you see coming from on high when you are working," she explained.

"One day, they brought me a girl nineteen years old. The doctors in the capital said she'd die. In Valencia they said the same. A *compadre* of mine recommended me to her family and so they brought her here, vomiting blood. I smoked a *tabaco* and saw that she was probably possessed, so we took her to the mountain and made a *velación*. My *banco* was Nieves but it turned out that day she was sick with a tumor on her head and I had to do it all on my own! I became possessed by a queen, *la reina* Yermina, who belongs to the Buchicaluri mountain, and then by the queen Margarita who also belongs to the Indian court. The first queen expelled the spirit causing the sickness. The second gave the names of the medicines necessary, and the girl got better."

Virgilio was nowhere to be seen.

As for Nieves, the doctors said surgery was impossible. They could only use drugs. It was left to Zaida to do the surgery, which she carried out successfully thanks to the spirit of José Gregorio. Later Zaida carried out operations for hernia and cancer of the liver but gradually that came to a halt. "Little by little, if you work with the spirits they will kill you. Finally I understood that spirits are ultimately treacherous and I had become an instrument of malignity."

Mission thought he understood, more or less. Hadn't Virgilio told him several times while bumping along in his taxi to the mountain that Zaida had gotten sick in the throat and they had gone from doctor to doctor, forced to sell their truck, their livelihood, until one day in the city, she heard an evangelist from Puerto Rico and felt relief.

"It was like a sword being taken out of my back," she told him. And she realized there and then that her illness was on account of her being possessed and that she would have to renounce her calling. Henceforth the mountain and all it stood for was the work of the devil. But where did that leave Virgilio with his devouring passion for the mountain?

Days later Nieves explained — in company with her brother who had been struck on the head by a falling beam years before, rendering him capable of not much more than accompanying his mother to the evangelical temple twice a day — that her father and mother were essentially separated, even though they lived under the one roof. It had been like that a long time, ever since Virgilio's lover, a woman who lived but a couple of blocks away, had made it impossible, using magic, for him to sleep with Zaida. What's more this woman had been persecuting Zaida for a long time — years before Zaida's first experience with spirits.

Zaida joined in. Yes! For years before being possessed she had felt she wasn't free. She felt humiliation. She felt strange things happening to her.

So Mission found himself drifting back to Quiballo, back to scenes under gloomy trees dripping with the mist of the mountain. He went with Nieves his mind full of wonder waiting for Ofelia, some vaguely familiar being to better take the measure of the unfamiliar. He knew some day she'd turn up.

And that day he was lucky.

She had just come back from Spain, from the Canary Islands, to be exact, on account of her having cured a madman.

She didn't carry out the actual cure in Spain but here on the mountain! She waited till he was asleep in the Canary Islands and then became possessed right here by the *Indio* Tamanaco, the Indian spirit pictured as a head severed by the Spanish. But it was a tough slog,

TAMANACO

TAMANACO

Cacique que fuiste decapitado y ahorcado por el bien de los tuyos ayúdame en estos momentos de penuria por los que atravieso ayúdame a salir bien, cobíjame con tu dicha de bondad y misericordia y que siempre tenga salud, dinero y felicidad. Por medio de tu dicha.
Amén.
Prenda una vela y rece un rosario

she had to admit, shaking her head, to get the spirit of an Indian to do this. The last thing an Indian spirit wants to do is cure a Spaniard.

She used her son as her *banco*. The cure succeeded so well that the madman's family invited her to their home in Spain. They were rich and owned a fine restaurant. She showed Mission fotos. In trance Tamanaco had shown her that it was the madman's aunt who had done him in out of envy of her sister's wealth. The madman's mother was shocked. "Yes!" concluded Ofelia. "There are many healers from here in the Canary Islands working with the spirit queen."

She had not only come back. She even owned one of the shacks, the big one at the end of the row.

Built of tin, the lofty shack was like a barn. It contained a restaurant with four tables, a fridge for pop and, at the back of the restaurant occupying almost a third its space was the most encumbered, the most extravagant shrine imaginable. Ofelia had put it together! Ofelia!

It was overwhelming. It tore into you from a dozen different angles at once, like a stage peopled by spirits of all shapes and sizes and radiant colors, casting shadows, emerging from shadows each one when it caught the eye decentering the tableau hitherto formed. Mission's eye dwelt on the four feet high plaster-cast figure of the spirit queen, pale faced but cheery in a vermilion robe and crown of gold, golden ornaments, and a large gold crucifix suspended from her neck by a cord of the national colors. At her feet was a plaster effigy of the Three Potencies with herself in the center and there was another plaster cast of herself in a blue gown holding a pink satin bow with statues of the *Indio* Guaicaipuro and *El Negro* Felipe on either side. There was Christ in a purple gown and wreath of thorns carrying a huge black cross. To his side was a bronze colored statue of a naked spirit queen, brawny thighs astride a sharp snouted jungle rodent, a copy of the statue erected in the center of the freeway in the capital outside the university at the time of the dictator in the early 1950s. Beneath them were Vikings draped diaphonously in satins of the nation's colors in shiny helmets and long blond beards, and there were at least two versions of Lino Valle, the renowned herbalist and hermit, one above the other in a little wooden cabinet with glass doors, one in a brown suit and tie, the other in his hermit's outfit sucking on a cigar, as may have been his wont those long lonely years in the magic mountain. Doctor José Gregorio Hernández was there as always, meek and debonair, clutching his stethoscope, together with many *africanos* seated regally amid heads of Indians, men and women, some with war bonnets — all draped with ribbons and candles and cloths of red and purple with brilliant purple flowers of all colors and sizes scattered around. There were two large prints of Jesus on the tin wall and a curious grey print of swirling water in a costly frame. It was a gift from a Muslim in gratitude for a cure. It contained verses from the Koran.

Ofelia had come a long way since the humble trip up the mountain in 1983 to the palace of the Liberator.

But then, so had Mission.

Emboldened by Ofelia's serenity as much as by the magnificence of her shrine, Nieves got more talkative. Her voice so plaintive ran on like the water trickling past the shrines as the gloom of Quiballo thickened like pea soup. But clearly etched in the shadows was the figure of the father and her concern for him. It was an old tale and her voice was tired. They had tried everything to no avail.

He drank too much and the root of the problem was the fact that his mistress had cast a spell on him using his sperm such that he was unable to have sexual relations anymore. Obsessed with his potency, he had spent a small fortune, close to 500 US dollars, injecting himself with medicine used to make stallions virile, to the point that he'd recently gotten a permanent erection requiring surgical intervention to release the congested blood.

And he's still injecting himself.

"It's dangerous work," commented Ofelia.

But then hadn't Virgilio said, face aglow, "I die, but the nation is saved!" on hearing Antonio Ricaute's name, the name of the leader, the hero on horseback? Wasn't the Liberator always monumentalized, fixed permanently in bronze and marble, erect on a stallion as depicted in Virgilio's carefully kept school-book? Wasn't it all so decidedly, so grotesquely, fitting, therefore, that Virgilio, too, especially because he wasn't really allowed out to the mountain any more, would inject himself with stud-enhancing elixirs in some sort of insane mock-ritual of spirit possession that in its very extremity oscillating back and forth between spleen and ideal stunningly expressed the anxiety of the state, struggling to regain emission-control?

Who knows? Maybe it would have been different if the mountain had stayed in the realm of the forest of symbols and the natural correspondences — in the hands of the three Virgins and Lino Valle, the hermit-professor; just voices emanating from the trees, far from horses and the seminal magic of heroes?

PART TWO

THE LIBERATOR'S COURT

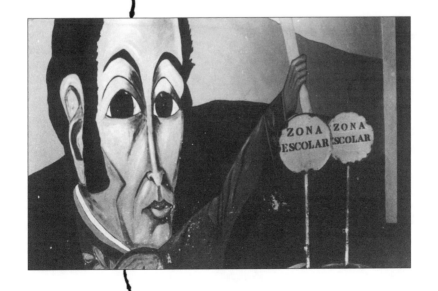

9 — The Infinite Melancholy

Virgilio wasn't supposed to go to the mountain. Not any more. Not just because of what had happened to Zaida but because of the hold the mountain had over him, keeping him captive, as much fascinated as scared. Now when he went he stood on the outside, as a spectator, timid, not like before when he was with his godfather, the holy hermit, professor Lino Valle. Now he peered through a lens darkly. Now he saw shapes and phantoms that weren't there before.

It was Mission who provided him with an excuse to go there. Nevertheless, it was with reluctance that he nursed the old Ford out of the plaza dedicated to the Liberator and down the maze of one-way streets, bakeries, shops of magic and ugly cinder-block houses on the road to the mountain. He always took his grandson with him. Maybe because he liked going there. Maybe because Zaida made him as a way of keeping an eye on things.

Zaida had the broadest face Mission had ever seen. When she smiled her face spread to the four corners of the world and from her eyes poured the stars of heaven. She had not one tooth. For eight years she had been a famous healer in the mountain.

The first she'd ever heard of the spirit queen was when she came in the early 1940s to live in this town close to the foot of the mountain. But, she emphasized, nobody worked in this sort of thing then. Nobody went to the mountain. Lino Valle, who later became famous as a herbalist, Celestino Soto, and Rodrigo, they were the first *médicos* to go out there. What's more in those days the *médicos* did not become possessed! Lino Valle would call the spirits with his mind and they would answer — but not through his mouth! Oh no! He had his hand over his mouth. Just a voice would come through the trees giving an explanation of the illness. The *médico* never talked. Just sat to one side and someone wrote down what the voice said.

It was years later, in the mid-sixties, she thought, that people started getting possessed. People from the cities. From the capital. There were none of these courts they have today around the spirit queen. Not even the *Indio* Guaicaipuro. Don Juan de Quiballo, don Juan de Sorte, don Juan de Yaracuay, they existed. Sure. Not even the Three Potencies existed and there was none of this stuff with the flag. What's more, people have gotten the spirit queen all wrong. In reality she has masses of blonde hair.

Mission was shocked. Masses of blonde hair! The founding figure of the violence founding the pathos of the nation — according to Zambrano, the fat professor out at the mountain — had masses of blonde hair! The ancient Goddess of these hot lands and mountains tumbling into crystal seas and ferocious Caribs — according to Katy and God knows how many anthropologists — the essential feminine and heart-bursting confluence of rite and history, had masses of blonde hair! Zaida certainly added a new note. She saw newness, not oldness, and the source of inspiration as lying not in the mountain but in the city. Living in the shadow of the mountain she was the authentic de-authenticator. She was from there. They were from elsewhere. She was like a rock. Not a flabby mystical bone in her. No glassy eyed mumbo-jumbo from her. And when she smiled, the four corners of the world lit up. It was a real smile. It gave freedom to the world.

Virgilio drifted into the conversation. He tended to disappear when he got home to this house of women but now his mind was spinning along the dusty mule path that led to the mountain in the late 1930s. In those days at the end of the path there were but three figures and they were the spirit queens: María Lionza, Isabela, and Margarita.

Don Juan de Sorte was around too. He was the uncle of María

Lionza. Oh! And then there was the spirit of don Martín Canete, from Coro. He was the godfather of María Lionza.

Virgilio differed from Mission in this way: he got history and spiritual anthropology straight from the spirits themselves. They would tell him who was who and where they came from and so forth. A living archive of the dead in the best positivist tradition. "Let the facts speak for themselves. And I mean speak."

How things had changed since he was young spinning along the dusty mule path to visit the queens, María, Isabela, and Margarita! Yet by what uncanny magic had something equally powerful been grafted onto that dusty journey known only to mules and hillbillies, something that gripped Virgilio with fervor equal to that reserved for the adoration of spirit queens. And not only Virgilio!

This other thing was the *Liberator thing*, and while it may have seemed strange to Virgilio to wake up one day and find the mountain abuzz with the festive opera of the state of the whole, he was himself by no means immune to the Liberator thing. Oh no!

Just a few days ago for instance Mission had been out at the mountain at Sorte with Virgilio and they'd passed the *portal* by the tin shacks and seen a newly placed beautiful statue of *El Negro Primero* with a bright medallion of the national colors painted on his chest. *El Negro* was decorously holding a picture of the *Court of the Liberator*, the white generals of the anti-colonial wars. At the center of the tableau was the Liberator.

Being of high status the spirits of the Liberator's court rarely, if ever, descend to possess the bodies of the living. But that day at Sorte, a little further on across the river and into the woods, Virgilio and Mission came across a magnificent *portal*, perhaps twenty feet across, vibrant with flaming candles, statues, portraits, and flowers. Overhead hung a huge and beautiful banner with the name José Antonio Páez embroidered on it.

After the Liberator, Páez was the most famous general of the founding violence of the founding fiction of the state of the whole. He was also his opposite in crucial ways — not upper class but a tough uncouth little guy with a barrel chest and brawny shoulders, not from the capital but from the grassy plains stretching back of the capital, first among equals in that knife-brandishing home of black cowboys. For a long time after the wars Páez' star ascended, while the Liberator died in exile by the sea, disillusioned and hated, his dream of liberation shattered.

There were maybe thirty young people milling around, law school graduates come to support their friends who had just graduated. The chief was very short — maybe as short as Páez himself — a bright alert woman from the capital, aged forty-two, with red, dyed, hair. Her enthusiasm and generosity were boundless.

Although born in the capital and with no connection to the countryside her ruling passion, and destiny, one might say, was to become possessed by spirits from the great plains, those same plains associated with Páez, his generals, and their fiercely devoted cowboys like the First *Negro* — *El Negro Primero* — whom Virgilio and Mission had seen as they entered the mountain that day, complete with his medallion of the national colors and the picture of the Liberator's court.

And it was real plainsmen that possessed her! Warriors, she insisted. More than one hundred years old, she insisted, such as José Antonio Páez, José Tomás Boves, and Antonio Ricaute. Great Men. Leaders, even if on opposite sides of the anti-colonial wars and the wars within those wars and dedicated to killing each other.

"I die. But the nation is saved," Virgilio whispered, on hearing Antonio Ricaute's name.

He began to talk about the anti-colonial wars. More like a litany. Unstoppable. The man was a walking encyclopedia, a high priest dedicated to the memory of leaders and battles. Bringing them back to life. And he'd only had five years' schooling.

Eventually he finished. "What happened with the Liberator," he said drawing in his breath, "was a thing of perfection. The same as God."

In front of the *portal* a woman asked for a broad skirt. Her voice was that of a poor Black. She was shaking violently. She had become possessed by the Liberator's wet nurse and began to draw human forms on the ground with talc. One by one she set the scantily clad young lawyers gently down. They fell into a deep sleep. Her shaking continued. She kept collapsing.

No resiste, whispered Virgilio.

She was lowered to the ground. Now the little chief entered the circle. She too had become possessed. She grabbed a stick. Someone passed her a broad brimmed hat. Stalking around the clearing. A transformed being. Lips pursed. Chin up. She was speaking in a strange accent — the accent of a tough plainsman with her red silky jacket, cross of Caravaca beautifully embroidered onto the back. Protection plus. She grabbed a lit cigar and set to, pummeling the abdomens of the lawyers lying in trance on the earth in front of the massive *portal*.

From a dark corner of his bedroom Virgilio lovingly extracted and dusted down a dog-eared book, *The Adventures of the Liberator: Autobiography*, by V. Romero Martinez. Bold letters declared First Edition 1972, with 12,000 copies, Second Edition the same year, 12,000 copies, Third Edition, 1973, 10,000 . The Fourth Edition dated 1976 was for 20,000 copies.

The first page was a facsimile copy of a typewritten letter from the Minister of Education of the state of the whole. The type of the typewriter stood out oddly from the rest of the book. It looked primitive and makeshift.

```
                   Be It Resolved
     By decree of the citizen President of the
     Republic and according to the rules of the
     technical organs of the Office, and in
     conformity with the disposition of Article
     63 of the General Rules of the Law of
     Education, The Adventures of the
     Liberator: Autobiography, is authorized as
     a complementary reading to be used in 4th,
     5th, and 6th grades of Primary Education
     as well as in the Basic and the
     Diversified Cycles of Middle Education.
```

The letter had a number stamped slightly askew on it.

No. 00146

The book was dedicated to Carmen,

my companion of light
a secure port in my journeys of affliction.

What followed were small chapters of text supposedly written by the Liberator during his adventurous life, each chapter denominated as "a step" and headed by an illustration.

The illustrations were curious. They were not pictures of the Liberator but were instead pictures of pictures of the Liberator, or pictures of statues of the Liberator. *Step 17* was headed by a crude drawing of a statue of the Liberator on a horse designed by an Italian and erected in Bogotá. *Step 20, "All Will Be Citizens"* was headed by a drawing of a statue in Lima, Peru, of the Liberator astride a rearing horse. *Step 10, "The Infinite Melancholy,"* was headed by a crude drawing of the Arc de Triomphe in Paris.

The emphasis in the illustrations of the second-order representations of the statued form ensured that his life was reduced — or should one say elevated — to monuments. This dialectic of reduction and elevation is worth noting because it manifests that salient property of the fetish — to register the representation rather than the being represented, the mode of signification at the expense of the thing being signified. Thus petrified, the statues, and even more emphatically the drawings of the statues, harvest a certain magic of death sustaining a concordance between meta-imagery and spirit-power.

Yet the result is that sometimes the comic element can be barely contained — and the fact that it *is* unstintingly contained in back-stiffening rites of recognition of founding fictions of identity is testimony to the public secret of the confluence of the official with the comic that makes kitsch an appropriate aesthetic for the magic of the state.

What has been described as the most distinguished literary commemoration of the Liberator's birth is Miguel Antonio Caro's *Ode to the Statue of the Liberator*, published in 1883 ("a ponderous but effective composition"). Not an ode to the Liberator. But to his *statue!*

At about the time this Ode to the Statue was being penned, the essayist José María Samper expressed his feelings of adulation in terms of a scheme in which "the Liberator I intend to describe is the Liberator I feel rise before my eyes like a colossal statue . . ."

This meta-ordering of representation serves to sharpen the appreciation for those of us magically protected from the magic spell that it is this barely achieved containment of the comic, more than the repression of true history, that gives the monument its fetish powers — the stupefying inability to laugh at what everyone secretly fears as the comic-absurd in the hysteria of the state's self-representation. For the great desire of the monument is its need for defacement.

As with the *Fuhrer* interpolating into the design of his monuments what he envisaged they would look like as ruins, the monument is erected as testimony to the sacred energy accrued by the stormy passage between sacrilege and sacrifice, between the demonic and the divine.

The problem is that while the art of this stormy passage seems to be second nature to the magicians and sorcerers who have peopled history, it is not all that easy for modern state machinery to pull this off without looking gauche or stupid. Given the power involved, however, nobody dares laugh, not just for fear of reprisal, but precisely because of the power that arises from just this risk of absurdity.

And what was noteworthy with Virgilio's textbook was not only representation through monumentalization, but the *crudity* of the representation and the coexistence of such crudity with *intimacy*.

There is a kind of power, as with kings and queens, saints and gods, in which baseness and transcendence circle around each other so as to produce power in the play of the shadow cast by the other. Greek gods known for their all too human foibles. Trouble is you can't tell when they are going to be aloof and when they are going to foible and descend from the Olympian heights. The famous "arbitrariness of power" refers directly to this bewildering mastery of baseness. In England they adore the queen. When she goes a-visiting shaking hands and entering some poor working class person's parlor, the people say Why! She's so human! They feel pleasure at her simplicity, at her being *down to earth*. More than pleased, elated. Something very special has happened. People never cease commenting on this "coming down." It virtually defines upness, royalty, that is. In fact they are more than pleased and more than elated; they are deeply mystified and moved by the mystery in ways regal and base. But this mystery they don't express, puzzled by this strange capacity of loftiness to stoop. Tactility has a lot to do with it. To be touched by royalty! At least by a king. Used to cure tuberculosis, known as the "king's evil." Note the meeting of opposites. Then the handshake. The solemn jerking up and down. Thesis, meet Antithesis. Pumping up the dialectic until faces melt in genuine smiles as eyes lock in dark pools of recognition. Fleetingly. Sure worries the hell out of the President's security detail, however, no matter how fleeting. He just won't stop shaking them hands. Voice gone. Arm gone. But still smilin'. And that irresistible urge they have to see the queen indecorous, on the shitter for example, standard trope, like Bataille fascinated by the urge to laugh in the presence of the corpse. One can only laugh at the mock solemnity of the face of those who work in funeral parlors. No monument is baseless.

Such dialectical pumping is essential to statecraft.

Its generative impulse feeds out into the world as the *effect of the official.*

The very crudity of the reproductions ensured this — just as the slightly askew positioning on the No. 00146 and the primitiveness of the typography of the letter from the Ministry of Education of the state of the whole enhanced the perfection of the official.

Then there was the austere language (in this book destined for children, remember) of the captions in a studious oficialese. *Step 20, "All Will Be Citizens,"* headed by a drawing of the statue of the Liberator on a rearing horse; the caption in bold letters reads "Adán Tadolini: Equestrian Monument of the Liberator, Plaza of the Liberator, 1874; copy of the original in Lima, Peru, inaugurated in 1858."

Important to this no-nonsense language is what at first sight might seem a foreign element, a quality of magical animation with which studious officialese is complicit in rendering the idolatry latent in monuments. In the case of Virgilio's textbook, magical animation is stimulated by the voice of intimacy pervading the text by means of the Liberator himself speaking directly to the schoolchild with easy familiarity all the way from the other side of the grave or, should we say, from the National Pantheon. It's like having the world reduced to a little voice perched inside your ear, the voice of God, the voice of your conscience, a flea biting in human words right where your sensate inside meets the big world outside rolling one into the other in a burst of spirit possession as the Liberator speaks inside you becoming you in a confessional tone, baring his soul, releasing it for other destinies.

And he seems tired as if he knew his words and image would be endlessly copied, worn traces of life to be worn by future generations. Dusting the cover so carefully, Virgilio seemed more like a nurse, more like a mother, gently wiping away the sorrow of the man whose image, like Prometheus' liver, was bound to never-ending sacrifice of consumption and reproduction. And what are we to make of the old man taking such loving care of a book for children? Is it not precisely in this that we might discern the tap-root of the magic of the state, no less than of the effect of the official — not merely in the combination of death with the child, but in the adult's imagination of the child's imagination?

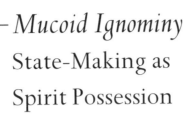

—*Mucoid Ignominy*
State-Making as
Spirit Possession

Even as he was being apotheosized in the capitals of Europe and the United States, he died in exile with but a handful of companions, coughing his tubercular lungs out on the hot coast at Santa Marta. He who had commanded enormous armies and beaten Murillo's Spanish cavalry into the ground. He who had changed the destiny of an empire and brought to a new world new nations. Acclaimed as The Liberator, within a few brief years his fame evaporated under a tropical sun.

But by some strange detour of the historical imagination the European Elsewhere resuscitated him a decade later. And boy! Did they resuscitate him! Statues were ordered from Paris and the US. Ships creaked with the weight of marble. It was prodigious. The return of the repressed, not to mention the insistence on recovering his remains from the spanking new republic to the west where he had laid his beleaguered bones to rest. But of rest there would be little. They wanted his remains, they insisted on his spirit, and in the absoluteness of the claims to the righteousness of possession they defined the very notion of nationhood. "Nobody has the right to go and get 'em but the nation to whom they belong," said General Páez to Congress in 1842, twelve years after the Liberator had died, heaped in vituperation from the very same Congress.

It was, in other words, the foundational act of spirit possession by the new state.

A boat named *The Constitution* was sent along the coast. Simón Camacho, part of the delegation, met with the young French consul and physician Próspero Révérend, who had been in Santa Marta since 1828 and had attended the Liberator in his last days and kept as a relic all those years a small piece of dried-up bronchial mucus retrieved from the Liberator's lung at postmortem, "with a somewhat oblong shape," commented Camacho, "porous and similar to the tiny bones to be found in the spines of fish."

It was with boundless appreciation that Próspero Révérend hung onto this dried mucus wrapped in the same paper it was put into at autopsy twelve years before. He planned to send it to France in case he died far from his family. Thus from hand to familial hand and through those hands from nation to nation, the anticipation if not fear of death serves to transfer the mucus of the man coughing to death in exile. Could there be a bond more intimate between nations than that established by this exchange of oddly shaped mucoid ignominy excavated from the corpse? And by what strange logic of taboo and transgression, by what strange mixture of medical license and ritual lore, could an act of such perfectly base materialism come so naturally to glorify the state of the whole?

Spirit-possession assumes continuity not so much after as through death, yet there is reason to believe the dying man had himself lost all hope of release, all hope of continuity. "It's ungovernable," he said. "Those who have served the revolution have plowed the sea." He saw himself captive of a fate no less inspissated than the Frenchman's little fetish. No Exit. The Illusion of Liberty. Death swarms here as a constant ferment rather than as closure. "How will I ever escape from this labyrinth?" he asked, when advised to call a priest for the last sacraments.

"And you," he asked Doctor Révérend, "what did you come looking for in these lands?"

"Freedom."

"And did you find it?"

"Yes, my General."

"Well, you were more fortunate than I, for I've still not found it. Go back to France . . ."

And one night they heard him say "Let's go! Let's go! . . . they do not want us in this land. Let's go, boys! . . . bring my luggage on board."

Yet those who came for his body years later were determined to find continuity. Camacho even heard the dead man speak (like Lino Valle under the trees with his hand over his mouth) and we who come still later than those twelve years of erasure, and exile — we who come long after those splendid formative years of oblivion followed by a century and a half of monumentalization no longer in mucus but in bronze and marble and plaster of paris — do we now need to be instructed as to the importance to the state of the whole of death, of the spiritual foundations of stately being as organized in the halo spreading out from the dead?

It was not all that different from the "second funeral" that the French ethnologist Robert Hertz described for so-called "primitive societies." In the first funeral, the body is disposed of until the liquids drain and the flesh withers to yield the white purity of the skeleton. Then, for the second funeral, months or years later, with due pomp and circumstance the ritualists get to work with bony renewal of the hopes and fabulations of the group as a whole, plummeting into the scenography of a wildly rent cosmos. At this point death may well ramify into carnival against a glorious backdrop of transgression and even sexual license, but with the Liberator this turmoil of death was instead recruited for the perfection of brooding mystery, the fatherland draped in black crepe with cannons booming "lugubriously," guns held vertically to the shore, vessels "furrowing the waves in a silence broken only by the creaking of the oars and the murmur of the waters." The people of the capital were joyful in their sorrow as they saw the remains "entering their native land with slow step and funereal trappings."

But as we look at the fate of this body of the father stronger in death than when he was alive, we discern another body forming, not only of joy as well as of sorrow but of an underground grotesque as the body comes to be divided between the state and the people, interlocking entities hovering indeterminately between being and becoming in the glow of each other's otherness, irradiated by increasingly sacred remains.

For the continuous coming-into-being of the state rested, in other words, on the continuous passing away of the body of the Liberator into the body of the people, and this constant passing-away itself depended on a capacity not merely to continuously resurrect his image, but to be possessed by his spirit by virtue of that image.

The image has therefore to bring back the dead, yet also signify their no longer being. Perhaps nowhere is this more strikingly acknowledged than with the common magical image obtainable for a few cents in *perfumerías* and marketplaces across the republic, the image of what we might call meta-death entitled "Fragment of the Testament of the Liberator" in which he himself speaks his release of body and soul as he is dying. It is not only testimony to his speaking his dying, but testimony to the genius of this popular culture to have seized on this image to drive home the power of a specific presence within dissolution and of course spirit possession accentuates this circuit of being and nothingness by performing it.

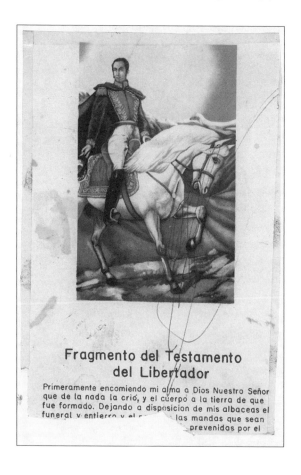

Fragmento del Testamento del Libertador

Primeramente encomiendo mi alma a Dios Nuestro Señor que de la nada la crió, y el cuerpo a la tierra de que fue formado. Dejando a disposicion de mis albaceas el funeral y entierro y el ...   ... las mandas que sean
                                   prevenidas por el

Here is where death, mediating the spirit of the state with the body of the people, meets its toughest task without which there would be no language; the task of giving life to the coming and going of figuration itself. Death accentuates the imaginative possibilities given in the shadow-play in the state of the whole; it provides the lurch of reality into the unknown that underlies every magical transformation from figure to figure of speech.

In his delirium he spoke of his exile: 'Let us go; bring my luggage on board. They do not want us in this country. Let us go.' The ship that was to bear him away lay waiting in the harbor—it was the ship of the dead. On December 17, 1830, at one o'clock, he embarked on his final journey to a land of glory—a glory that has grown as the shadows grow when the sun is declining.

This passage comes from a painstaking German refugee historian writing during World War II. It remains the most respected scholarly account of the life of the Liberator, "The ship that was to take him lay waiting in the harbor—it was the ship of the dead."

Let us look at this ship. Where is it waiting? Where is it going? What sort of journey does it provide? This ship is the ship of figuration. It is death itself, and while nothing could be more literal than the corpse, harbinger of nothingness, yet it is the very concreteness of this *finis* which provides the ship with its amazing capacity for travel. Death takes a hold of the biographer, too, possessed in this instance by his imaginings—of extremity, exile, delirium, and death impending in the wake of brutal colonial war reaching its climax in eventual victory and world-scale historical change. The material rushes forward directing the otherwise sober pen staging the scene "on board"—on board what? "The ship that was to bear him away lay waiting in the harbor." One sees the vessel waiting, rocking at anchor in the deep blue of the bay, wood and canvas straining, empathetic with the exiled man's despair and self-pitying practicality—only to have this reality torn from its moorings, for this is no ordinary ship, my friend, this is both bigger and less than life. "It was the ship of the dead." Thus we rock back and forth, straining at anchor. The need for the object, the object that was.

Yet not all the bodily remains made it to the new state of the whole. It is said that the new nation from where the remains were removed asked to keep one thing, the heart, and that it was buried in an urn at Santa Marta.

Yet this heart has never been found.

And how could it be found? After twelve years there would be no heart nor much of anything else.

The fantasy-*extraction* of the heart from the corpse is on a par with the "fact" that the buried heart has "*disappeared*," because it is the absence of the material yet mortal element—its contrived nothingness and its forgotten somethingness—that generates spiritual release. It is this that sweeps the biographer once more into the vortex of figure and flesh, metaphor and body as he, too, possessed by the spiritual power of the image of the absent thing replicates in words the performance of spirit-possession when he writes that this incident is a symbol of the process whereby the Liberator entered the realm of myth. "*His heart is not underground, confined within walls of clay,*" he wrote. "*It lives and beats in every South American breast.*"

This sentence burns across the page. Just a metaphor, you might say, as if metaphor were not essential to the artwork by which the sense of the literal is captured. Imagine the fellows removing the heart and burying this "metaphor," literalizing the idea, fortifying spirit. Or imagine the fellows who said there were such fellows, or the fellow who wrote the above words in which myth and figure slip through the materiality of the heart of the dead man to enter hyperrealism. Above all imagine your imagining's effect on the poetic resource of language and spirit where substance dies to release figuration.

Imagine also a full century before these words were written of impossible organs disappearing and reappearing in spirit bursting through underground caverns of clay, imagine that other young fellow, Simón Camacho stepping off the deck of *The Constitution*, charged likewise with the conversion of substances into sacred power, but this time at the founding point—gathering human bones together with a medley of sanctifiable impressions inured to salt air, dry heat, and red dawns creeping over the cool patios of the Spaniard's flat-roofed hacienda a mile or so in from the bay of Santa Marta at the foot of the Sierra Nevada where the Liberator had died, blending, making a picture, setting a death scene woven together with a selection of memories as if making an amulet.

But this was no ordinary amulet, this resurrection of the very idea of the state, so empowering its force, so forever beyond representation as testified to by the hysteria of replication thereafter. And how did he do it, this young Camacho? Of course he was just a cog in the machine, and an old machine, at that, adapted to particular conditions where Church and State, magician and warrior, had to shake themselves loose from the turmoil of colonial war so as to reconstitute a sacred basis of power from the second funeral, the one that counts.

The Second Funeral: Surrounded by slums and violence in a beautiful single-story colonial house with wide verandas and Mediterranean tiles covered with moss under sprawling eucalyptus trees is one of the many museums of the Liberator, a virtual shrine, on the walls of which are three astonishing prints of the entry or planned entry of the Liberator's bones into the capital. These illustrations are reproduced in Camacho's memoir as well, and it seems that they were the basis for the ritual design of the formative moment of the new state — the design itself concocted in Paris. And who was sent to Paris to oversee the construction of the magical vehicle in which the sacred remains would enter the capital, the making of the Arch of Triumph it would pass through, and the magnificent purple velvet draperies in the temple where the remains would be placed? None other than the Italian, Augustín Codazzi, the man whose task it was to map the new nation and in this manner affix its boundaries if not its virtuality.

The central feature of this state-making apparatus was the huge phallus, the catafalque, created to receive the Liberator's remains. Standing about fifty feet high, its prepuce of soft tasseled drapes flowed down to severe steps on which stood three "Indian" men around a bare-bosomed woman crouching at the foot of the erection.

Sure, the French physician, Próspero Révérend, had, thanks to the abject holiness the corpse stimulates, gotten some inspissated mucus at postmortem, and God knows how many people from Haiti to Lima might soon be claiming they had some of the Liberator's hair. Sure, Virgilio is at work injecting himself with stud-enhancing fluids, eyes shining with the utter perfection of the Liberator thing. But this monument to carry the Liberator's bones was not just body-parts and fluids teetering on the threshold of quaint ritual endeavor. This was in altogether another league — the culmination where death engorged the primal organ of statehood sprouting from Indianness, shooting forth silver stars over cascading veils and palls of purple velvet with gold arabesques.

Truth or fantasy-truth? Did this state-making-thing really exist outside of its representation? What is certain is the accuracy of the idea shooting forth in its second and repeated comings following the originary act of spirit possession by the state arising from the ashes of war. And this war is ceaseless.

On June 4th, 1987, there appeared in the daily newspaper, *The Universal*, an article under the title "President Lusinchi Baptized Two Works on the Liberator." Included was a photograph of the nation's president standing beneath a statue of the Liberator—identical to the statue that stands by the side of the spirit queen at the foot of the enchanted mountain. Like a priest, the President is baptizing two books on the Liberator, one from which I have been quoting in the foregoing pages by Gerhard Masur, the other by August Mijares, both reprinted jointly by the Office of the President of the Republic and the National Academy of History, the Mijares volume being given a print run of 100,000 copies that, according to the article, would be massively distributed.

"We want to take the Liberator to the depths of our people," says the President. "We want to use the Liberator. And I feel confident he would feel good as our instrument of politics when he is being weakened by political forces. In action as well as thought the Liberator was a man who struggled to make our peoples a brotherhood. In public he always stood for a Latin American and ecumenical vision. He was a universal man, an extraordinary man, and for this he lives on."

If the President himself is represented in the cupola of public space as baptizing lives of the Liberator and as feeling confident that the Liberator feels good, if Presidential discourse assumes the vital, moody presence of this divine spirit, validating it as a force that not only *lives* in the present but to a crucial extent *makes* it as well—then it requires little imagination to slip into the no less fantastic work of the spirit-medium, Ofelia, by the Liberator's palace and waterfall on the spirit queen's mountain saying, in her work-a-day way, that this very same spirit is good for business, money, and things of government.

She too is harvesting the abundance flowing from the power of the story of a Nation-State etheralised in embodying the spirit of a dead man on horseback. The President deftly follows Ofelia in this, and she follows her President. This is the magic circle. He performs on behalf of the state, she on behalf of her distressed clients, mobilized by a staggered circulation of images and effervescent shocks—one of the most startling of which in the national scheme of things is the attempted *golpe militar* or military coup, the most recent of which, led by a Colonel Chávez who was imprisoned shortly thereafter, inspired the following incantation to be circulated on the busy streets of the capital:

Our Chávez who art in prison
Hallowed be they name
Thy people come
Thy will be done
Here
As in your army
Give us today the lost confidence
And never forgive the traitors
As we ourselves will never forgive them
Who betrayed us
Save us from corruption
And liberate us from the President

Amen.

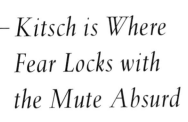

II — *Kitsch is Where Fear Locks with the Mute Absurd*

His image is everywhere—on the walls, on the stamps, on the schools, on the money, on the mountain tops, on the prisons, and in the center of every town and hamlet any and everywhere. The young priest from Spain shakes his head. The old men come by and take their hats off as they pass his statue in the plaza. They call him a saint! They ask me to perform a mass for him! For a dead man. Yes! I will do that. But as a saint! Never!

But, what's more important here, the image or its ubiquity? The image, or the obsession at work in this frenzy for duplication and display that leaves the Church shaking?

In an essay entitled "The Exemplary Life of the Liberator" published in 1942 we read:

> *Every moment you hear the name of the Liberator. His name appears daily in the newspapers, innumerable times. His portraits are beyond counting, his face, his profile, his entire body, his bust. Painted in color or in black and white; in sumptuous frames or humble strips of cedar, on horseback in apostolic triumph; on foot, sword at his side; in soldier's uniform, in civil dress; with papers, sign of the legislator. Fixed with thumb tacks to the wall; in the homes of the rich, in the hut of the peasant standing on the mountain against the blue sky or the green of the countryside. His face, grave and pensive, is unforgettable. In postage stamps he's on the letters of your parents, your brothers and sisters, your friends, your own. He's on the white silver coins and on the shiny yellow golden ones. If you go to a public office, you'll find him there in a central place, together with the flag and shield of the Fatherland. The central and most elegant plaza of the greatest city of our country is called the Plaza of the Liberator. And in almost all the towns of our country where there is but one plaza, it is called the Plaza of the Liberator. If there is no more than one constructed, it will bear the name of the Liberator . . .*

And so it continues.

It must seem sometimes as if the entire country has been converted into a mausoleum with statues of the Liberator nailing down the state of the whole good and tight; all this naming and picturing and retelling in words and stones, paint and bronze, all this effort visible through imagery bespeaking some enormous love if not unshakable anxiety, all this *effort*, and not just the goal itself, this constant commitment to the image as begun by Congress in 1842 — the untiring ubiquity of it all so serious that one can only laugh, then freeze struck dumb by fear of some nameless retribution, precisely this moment of free-fall that is sacred.

MINISTRY OF CULTURE

> *He waited all afternoon at the Ministry of Culture for a letter to research the archives concerned with the construction of memorials of the anti-colonial wars and of the death of the Liberator. There were a lot of people waiting and it felt like a dentist's waiting room, only the people walked around and were more nervous. A young man complained bitterly that he was a composer of music but nobody wanted to listen to his recently composed requiem to the Liberator because the Liberator's not dead.*

The magic in this figure of remembrance, and believe me there is plenty, is testimony to a surplus of effort spilling over the edges of the object of retrieval itself, a sort of state-inspired vast vomiting of His image akin to the destruction entailed in sacrifice, making holiness through the extravagance of deliberate loss. The image is no longer the man, but expenditure itself.

Likewise, possession in this European Elsewhere drives the eye to the spirit resurrected. To the image. That is certainly true. But even more important than the figure remembered, yet intimately blended with it in consummate complexity and intensity, is the sensational flourish in the act of possession itself, in what we might call the excess involved in imageric splendor.

His image is everywhere. But this is no panopticon of visual pursuit, no visible or invisible eye perusing you wherever you are wherever you go.

If anything it's the reverse. This is an eye more like the Sacred Heart of Jesus festooned with thorns and set beating maladroitly in the middle of His chest setting up some hypnotic image which demands being looked at and, in that exchange of looks, obeisance.

Of course one does not really look, just as one does not really look at the sacred heart of Jesus. It's just there in its thereness because remembrance demands the image, loses itself in the image, and the image then proliferates as the populace through some strange compulsion seeks out his empty gaze in a pursuit doomed to eternity.

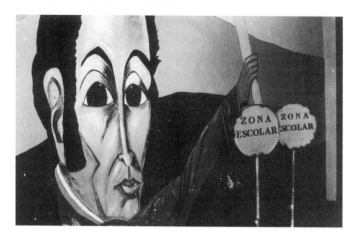

His image is everywhere, a controlled frenzy of kitsch across the cultured landscape, the bridges, the bus stops, the money, cigar wrappers . . . not to mention his statue centering every hamlet, village, town and city nailing it to the earth just as his horse spreads its wings skywards. No wonder the men raise their hats into the air. It's as if there is, finally, nothing . . . nothing to represent other than this effusion.

And this is no less fearsome than absurd, teetering on the comic, the fall from the commanding heights, hooves churning with sacred energy the mixture of fear and absurdity that is virtually inarticulable other than in self-consciously naive art adrift in the passing crowd, fixed momentarily by their gaze in the central plaza, or floating wavelike on the freeway.

There can be no better form of expression of the culture of the official than the blank nothingness of the eyes looking out at the populace in a conspiracy of silence that it's all a game, a stupid, necessary, terrible, and unholy game. One day he'll wink. The day after we're dead. This is most definitely not a laughing matter. Remember the young man in the Ministry of Culture? Whatever the cause of this taboo which exercises like all taboos the force of nature and the deities combined, it must at some point connect not only to a nameless fear of retribution but to an associated sense of awkwardness which trips the tongue into spasms of absurdity expending endlessly. The mountain of the spirit queen is the quintessence of this; with Quiballo it reaches perfection.

This silence cannot be broken — except for the slogans painted tirelessly on walls; walls of schools, inside and on the street-side, prisons, bridges, central plazas, police stations, bus stops . . . wherever a good wall comes along.

Verbal equivalent of the portrait, the slogan as oracular statement is also equivalent to the monument bringing together death, memory, and the state, only the slogan is more mobile as befits the modernity of the freeway age when sacred centers give way to nomadic movement from slogan to slogan. . . .

On the wall of the bank in huge letters:

IF NATURE OPPOSES US
WE SHALL FIGHT AND MAKE HER OBEY

Such are the immortal words of the Liberator, words now so much part of nature there is no need to control her. The ultimate fetish twist. And not just in the cities. On the wall of a sand-bagged police station by the side of a highway running through a remote hamlet, by the side of a portrait of the Liberartor, is painted:

THOSE WHO ABANDON ALL TO SERVE THE FATHERLAND
LOSE NOTHING & WILL BECOME ONE WITH THE SAINTS

From whence come these words? Who is speaking?

The questions are insistent. They fade away. Beneath lie neatly stacked sandbags ready for an armed attack.

From whence come these attacks?

And what shall we call them;

quotations?   revelations?

obsessions?   spells?

graffiti?   excerpts?

sound-bites?   advertisements?

slogans?

ONE IMPRUDENT STEP COULD BURY US FOREVER

In a remarkable passage (it now being my turn to quote) redolent with the majesty of its subject-matter and entitled "Invisible Crowds," Elias Canetti reminds us that "over the whole earth, wherever there are men, is found the conception of the invisible dead." The image here is of a vast and troublesome horde of dead pressing through time, immanent in the world's make-up, another element of nature, so to speak, like wind, rain, and stars. Drawing on ancient history and ethnography, Canetti conjures up the image of ghosts filling earth, sea, sky, rivers and forests — to which we must add the ghosts of freeways, bridges and tunnels — triumphs of modernity — no less than of postage stamps, and currency — talismans of state ensuring the ghostly web of the universal equivalent.

The invisible crowd obsesses the living to such a degree that it becomes an essential part of life itself. In Celtic, in the Scottish Highlands, Canetti quotes, the word for the invisible crowd of the dead is *sluagh*. The dead are restless. They fly about in great clouds like starlings, up and down the face of the world, returning to the scenes of their earthly transgressions. They fight battles as men do on earth and may be seen on clear and frosty nights, advancing and retreating, and after battle the rocks are stained crimson with their blood. The word *ghairm* means shout or cry, and *sluagh-ghairm* was the battle-cry of the dead. Later on this word became *slogan*, adds Canetti, who notes that "the expression we use for the battle-cries of our modern crowds derives from the Highland hosts of the dead."

Canetti attaches a lot of importance to the invisible crowd. He roams like a deadman himself through hosts of angels and saints clouding the skies of religions. "The minds of the faithful are full of such images of invisible crowds," he asserts, and he wonders if religions began with them.

So we move to an equation of faith bound to the obsessing presence of the invisible crowd–and as we move we may start to think of other sorts of crowds, the crowds of modernity into whom the power of the dead is transmitted–especially posterity in the form of the children, that perennially other crowd of starlings and protoplasmic creaturely potential in whose evocation so much state policy is justified.

For the circuit of meaning and bodily impulse diffusely uniting the official with the unofficial is nowhere more uplifting than with its use of the children and, more particularly, with its use of the deliberate confusion entailed by an adult-executed childish iconography of and for the state. Take this scene: an oversized glossy book published in the capital in the 1980's on the popular architecture of the country. Skillful colored photographs illuminate the pages. At the end there is a double-page layout. On the left hand side there is a cute picture of the national flag, presumably painted by a child, on the rough textured exterior wall of a house. On the right side we have the authors' commentary, which stands as the book's final words.

> *The popular is sincerity. The popular is obvious*
> *The popular is human, at times simple and crude, but human.*
> *Sentiments need no erudition . . .*
> *When a child paints the flag on the wall of a house and writes,*
> *"This is the flag of my country,"*
> *A great sentiment is revealed.*
> *What's important is what one has within; not the exterior,*
> *The popular is the spinal column of the nation.*

What's important is the inspired confusion of stately interchange between adult and child worlds. Take the Introduction to the ur-text of the state of the whole — the prescribed school text-book for junior grades, *My History of My Country: Basic Education*, published in the capital in 1986:

> *History is like a magic mirror in which we see reflected the face of our people in the past, the present, and the future. . . . We need to acquire consciousness of this collective face in our youth so it will always be with us, providing us with the opportunity to create and recreate our existence in the future.*
>
> *Strengthening this sense of belonging to our history and to our country makes for men tied by their umbilical cords to the historic process that has formed us at all times.*

The authorial voice in these opening pages of a book of instruction for children is ambiguously directed with all the cunning that the political unconscious can muster towards *both* child and adult, as if one adult, the author, is explaining and legitimating a particular pedagogical practice to another adult but necessarily within earshot of children who are put in the position of being included in their exclusion and excluded in their inclusion — as children usually are in/out of conversations between adults, the latter exchanging remarks and even confidences as if the children, although physically present, are mentally absent. (This achieves its most comical aspect when the adults "confidentially" lower their voices, causing the child, rendered invisible by childhood in this scenario, to pay close attention.) The point is that to the degree that this gives the child a fascinating epistemic position — part licensed eavesdropper, part idiot, part fairy — so it grants even more incredible possibilities to the artwork of the adult speaking for the state in the name of this child picturing the spirits of the dead. Stately being, we might say, thus achieves its most profound dimensions where the invisible crowd of the dead mingles with the adults' version of the child's imagination of that crowd.

This is where the naive finds its home, where the stately imagination of the imagination of the child abuts that of the death-space of colonial and anti-colonial violence as represented in some doll-like time out of polymorphously perverse toy-soldier time. The magic of the state lies not only in the space of death — as on the magic mountain of the spirit queen — but in a far more sinister fashion in varying combinations of inarticulable fear and absurdity uniting death and the children, as a glance at the daily newspapers of any country today will show.

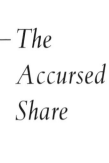

12 — The Accursed Share

In the circuit of exchange between the wink that's about to occur and the death that's imminent, in the exchange between the absurd and the official, the art of the naive and the ingenuous gathers its wherewithal, fast-frozen in the image on the wall of the school, police station, prison, *and* popular shrine. Here is where the crucial exchanges occur, the same exchange of powers that occurs between the spirit queen and the Liberator, icon of the state-founding violence of the anti-colonial wars now washed away in wave after wave of infantilizing kitsch, while she, in her nether-space of wildness and margination, in ways obvious and oblique, also maintains the presence of this founding violence.

But what is so revelatory, so fascinatingly revelatory, of course, is what it is about such founding violence that she brings out of the kitsch-shadows—all that is seductive and sinister in the fury for reduplication in the otherwise perky image of the man on the white horse stomping at the bit, pawing the ground.

Through the elusive partnership of the holy couple formed by the Liberator and the spirit queen, the negative sacred within the awe of the stately sublime is not so much hidden as it is *hiddenness performed*, an intermittently exposed public secret as to the submerged presencing of a feminized abject within the founding violence of Law represented by the Liberator astride his mountain of dead.

But sometimes we do not have to wait for the sudden revelation that comes from her awkward pairing with Him, because even in the circulation of His image *on its own* there can occur that rupture wherein the polluting powers of the uncanny emerge from Him, and do so unaided. For she has her mountain, but he is mounted — not only on horseback but on the walls of all official buildings such as displayed here inside the police station in the town closest to her magic mountain. Above the tv the wall is given over to the Liberator absorbed by the energy of his deep chested steed accentuated by the clefts of testicular shadows.

But who is in charge, the diminutive rider or the massive horse? The man seems to be sinking into the animal such that brute instinct becomes enshrined. The crudity of the drawing seems deliberate. After all, the usual official icon could have been used instead. The crudity suggests an attitude towards representation itself.

Perhaps this very crudity gets us closer to understanding what Walter Benjamin in his 1920 essay on the legal theory of the modern state referred to as the *spectral* being of the police in democracies — spectral on account of the way the police occupy and take advantage of a sort of no-man's land of violence between the making and the execution of law? Is it not a scary image? In part this could be because of its strategic incompleteness, because the painter, so the police say, has yet to finish his job as if, one day, the crudity will be absolved in a figure of sublime perfection. But is not this very unfinishedness the empowering sign of the diffuse never-endingness of ramifying mediation of the official in the unofficial, which is exactly where policing lies?

And if it is the function of this eruption of the sacred on the interior wall of the police station to mark and thus bear witness through me to you of this confluence, then we must also acknowledge a particularly scrotal primitivism and animal eroticism inevitably aroused in the confluence of violence and reason where the police, to an unnatural and monstrous degree, argues Benjamin, mix the violence founding law with the violence maintaining law. It is this monstrous mixture which gives to the police, he argues, their strategic formlessness, their "nowhere tangible, all-pervasive, ghostly presence in the life of civilized states." Not only ghostly, mark you, but rotten as well, the abject realm of the phobic object; spectral putrefaction in blue uniforms and brass buttons, neatly pressed khaki shirts, dark reflector glasses and bulletproof vests.

What then of the celebrated definition of the modern state as that which holds the monopoly of the (legitimate) use of violence? And what then of that equally celebrated definition stressing bureaucratized rationality? Are we forced to think not only of groups of armed men and prisons, and not only of stately pyramids of filing cabinets and rules and regulations, but also — and this is surely the whole and consuming point, where violence and reason blend — of ghosts and images and, *above all, of formless, nauseating, intangibility*? It would appear so, just as it appears that in its rottenness this very spectrality opens the door to magical rituals of reversal that capture the haunting power of the state so as to reverse fate itself.

Yolanda Salas de Lecuna tells us, for instance, that the police are said to magically invoke the Liberator to make themselves invisible when carrying out a dangerous mission, and that soldiers may use him to appear more numerous than they really are, thereby frightening the enemy away (the enemy being fellow citizens and immigrants, rarely the military of other sovereign states).

No matter that this may be "mere" folklore, popular fantasy as to what goes on in the hidden precincts of policing. To the contrary, in this way we are given a glimpse into both the production and nature of the magic of the state as paranoiac mystique; the *invisibility* of security forces and strategic *confusion* as to numbers and force of bodies of armed men acting in the name of the state. Not only are both these features commonly deployed components of real state power the world over, but, given the paranoiac penumbra continuously secreted by stately being, it is impossible to draw a line and say when these properties are magical and when they are not.

It is, moreover, along the wavy edge of this penumbra that the image-sphere penetrates the body, collective no less than individual — and precisely on account of this wavy-edged paranoid intensity, the image-body nexus of stately being is eminently susceptible to reversal through other sorts of surreal ritual. The paranoiac penumbra provides the spectral flux through which Leviathan, both god-like and monstrous, pivots his accursed face for these very same powers of confusion and illusion can be turned *against* the state and used by ordinary people so as to free prisoners and avoid military service (a state obligation prosecuted with considerable verve and public drama).

"The Liberator is able to save those who go to the army. You can ask this of him because he struggled and fought against the government. If one asks with all of one's heart that one's son not go to the army, he understands because he suffered too."

In a petition to the Liberator in the form of a prayer (what other form of petition could there be?) the spirit queen and other spirits of importance are implored to provide admission to his presence. The concluding lines . . .

For me and for my home
I ask permission to invoke
The spirit of the Great Liberator
Humbly pleading with all my heart
To concede me at this sacred hour this petition:
Lend me your armies of liberation
So as to conquer
All my enemies.

But for all the stress on armies, liberation, and conquest, it's not Force in some vitally crude sense of force of arms that is appealed to, but Confusion. For all the masculine stress on heroism in both state and popular culture, it would seem that *confusion*, the tool of the fox and the weak, is the primary tool to deploy against persecution.

Take this healer, in front of his shrine. He is asking the Liberator for protection, protection against persecution and envy. He is mixing essences. Three essences. They each bear a name and a color.

- Confusion,
- Tame the Strong (*Amanza Guapo*),
- Domination.

And it is the blue of Confusion, he says, which must predominate because it is Confusion (along with a portrait of the Liberator) that is the key ingredient in the engagement with persecution — persecution itself being understood as a species of dialectics, of intertwining confusions played off against counter confusions . . . and here is where the circulating image is crucial.

Like the face on the money that can release you from prison.

"In a person's home," says the healer, "first thing you'll find is a portrait of the Liberator. It's always there. He's not just a person who made history, but someone who did something great. . . . To begin with the system of mobilization is the money, so that when you need to overcome some problem, take hold of a palpable photograph of the Liberator, up to a large bill [of the national currency], and if you have a personal problem or someone from your family is in prison, take hold of the portrait of the Liberator, a glass of water, light a candle, and make your petition with devotion. Your problem will be solved."

"It's as if it really was the image of the Liberator that did it."

"Faith is necessary. Always."

It's as if state and people are bound to the immanence of an immense circle of magically reversible force, in effect a never-ending exchange of some ancient gift-like force that we will call *the accursed share* — the same exchange that draws the eyes of the citizen to the forlorn eyes of the Liberator, awaiting the wink the day after we're dead, the exchange that ripples back and forth between him and the spirit queen in the staging of hidden innerness — the exchange that not only allows reversibility but is built on its two-facedness as much as on death and the magic thereof.

That this is a story, the story of stately presence, should alarm nobody. For how could it be otherwise, the powers so powerful, the unities so binding, the circularity so perfect that in the end no less than in the beginning there shimmers the fantastic power of spirit engulfed in the objecthood of the body and the objecthood of the sword. Hobbes described this circulation of the accursed share in terms of a mythical covenant creating the state, a covenant made by everyman with everyman to escape the violence of the state of nature. Since covenants without the sword are but words, the covenant required that the violence of the state of nature be not only abrogated but given over to and made constitutive of this newly-emergent force in world history, thus qualifying for the title of the great Leviathan, that biblical monster which, although it had turned against God, was seen by Hobbes, in its standing for the state, as "that mortal god which is but an artificial man; though of greater stature and strength than the natural" — the point being that no matter how historically inaccurate this fable obviously is, it is nevertheless a telling account of the mythological principles inevitably and necessarily involved in modern state formation which no history can articulate, but which all histories require. In other words these stories of the coming into being of the state are not only fantastic history but — and here's the rub — precisely as fantasy are essential to what they purport to explain such that any engagement with the thing called the state will perforce be an engagement with this heart of fiction, the very script of whose real and grave purpose presupposes both theater and spirit possession.

Take the case of the realness of the accord that makes the state of the whole. The agreement between the state-making men "is more than consent or concord," says Hobbes, "it is a real unity of them all in one and the same person." But how can we understand the theory of representation — political and epistemological — in this *real unity* whose realness Hobbes is at such pains to emphasize, this unity that is "more than consent or concord"? It is more than symbolism or metaphor, it is so *real* a unity that the bodies themselves seem merged into and embodied by the one that represents them. This is so material that like the fetish it has to be mystical and language is insufficient here, other than the language of spirit; a language shaped for the articulation of paradox, for suspension of disbelief along the moving edge where the need to speak the unspeakable reigns jointly alongside the threat or actuality of socially validated violence. In short this is the language of embodiment of spirit, and the unity Hobbes seeks is both that of spirit possession and of theater as when he posits his contracting men as thus bound in the body of Leviathan as actors — therewith opening the state of the whole to other scenarios as the play of disguise no less than force and fraud emerges from the very interior of the rationality of contract.

Hence the performance art of the healer locking horns with the performance art constitutive of stately being — the healer with his "palpable photograph" taking a hold of the face of the Liberator in his theater of ritual reversal, absorbing the mythical powers of the social contract, engaging its violence with confusion, its confusion with counter-confusion, extracting the magic of the modern state thanks to a post-Hobbesian theory, we might say, of the postmodern state, but doubtless in great debt to Hobbes, to Hobbes' very spirit, we might say. It is not the healer who is mystical, but the state.

The circulation embedded in the covenant made by everyman with everyman is thus a curious and contradictory thing, a double and doubling-back haunted and abject state of the whole thing — but one that works and contains a secret known to all, not agreement so much as the agreement to agree, not belief so much as make-believe which, in retrospect, is but a formula of infinite regress checked by mythic power (of the covenant) providing, in sum, an expansive and indeed spectral field for fetishisms of body and sword around the word.

Fundamental here is the sword which, in the figure of Leviathan, is both internal and exterior to the element of gift exchange in the covenant wherein the violence of the state of nature becomes the auratic nature of the state. For although the sword is there only as a last resort, as threat it lives ever-present as the sublime, necessary for the maintenance of the contract which, to be effective, must be based on goodwill between the parties to the contract.

And what is momentous in this coagulation of force and goodwill is the gift involved in the metamorphosis required for state-making, the self-sacrifice of everyman's capacity for violence to that of the state. It must be Hobbes' argument that this gift is the epitome of reason.

Hobbes puts the words into the mouths of his contracting men: "I authorize and give up my right of governing myself, to this man or assembly of men, on this condition, that thou [too] give up thy right to him, and authorize all his actions in like manner." Rousseau is equally clear on what is more than a surrender, namely the gift-like quality, the giving quality, as when he speaks of the person *having to give himself to all*. "Each of us places his person and all his power in common under the supreme direction of the general will; and as one we receive each member as an indivisible part of the whole."

And like Hobbes, he sees the contract as sacred.

If we are to think of the surrender of the capacity for violence as a gift, and this gift as a sacrifice, let us be mindful of the notion of sacrifice as that which mysteriously makes sanctity and does so through destruction, often violent. "Sacrifice destroys that which it consecrates," wrote Bataille, and this is the necessary fate of *the accursed share* reserved for the gods and Leviathan alike. In Hobbes' version, the accursed share would be the violence of the state of nature handed over to the state by means of the inconceivably rational contract. Indeed, the very rationality of the contract that is covenant is dependent on the mystical sacrifice it contains, and in the European Elsewhere the accursed share is made manifest by the spirit queen's mountain as that which is both holy and unclean, sacred and forbidden, the dangerous "underside" of stately purity without which neither the Liberator nor Leviathan could represent the "real unity."

The Blue of Confusion is thus more than a tactical ruse in a running skirmish with the advance guard of stately prowess, for its power rests on what the spirit queen's presence reveals in the sacred covenant of stately being.

In using the image of the Liberator, the healer thus enters into what we might call the interiority of the famous covenant by which society at one stroke established itself and the state in the "scene" where gift and contract interpenetrate each other's being. Into this zone of the accursed share goes the healer, talking the language of ritual excess of good and evil apportioned the gods.

Such rearrangement of the terms in the covenant is hardly difficult because ritual reversal of the power in the image of the Liberator is always already there as potential in the image itself — as on the interior wall of the police station, and as brought to the surface by his pairing with the spirit queen who provides, in his shadow, as on the magic mountain, the dread and sacred powers of transgression that flow from entering what amounts to the mother herself by means of the shrines laid out along the body of the mountain that is the people.

But what sort of drama is this?

There is the drama of the circulation through the metamorphosis of the gift as in the sacred covenant whereby the general will *made itself* by *giving itself* over in a superior, concentrated, violence, to found both state and society.

There is the "totemic" drama intertwined with this of the obsessive memorialization of the founding violence enacted by the band of brothers creating Law in the shadow of the body of the mother which is what gives the advance guard of the Law, namely the police, their artfully confusing and spectrally blurred, even rotten, abject, quality, so suited to the play of magic and counter-magics.

But most fundamental and least noted of all by psycho-analysis and political philosophy is the drama beholden to the silent tension of the comic-absurd laced with fear, the unsayable that beams out of the eyes in the portrait of the Liberator from every wall, postage stamp, bank-note, and statue. It is this adult-executed childish iconography that propels the spirit-possession theatrics of caricature and literalization — as on the magic mountain — bringing metaphor and national history into the gesticulating human body. It is this iconography of the stately naive, combining the death-space with the child, that allows the visual fix of the image as on the money or on the wall of the police station to spiral off from the fearsome absurdity of the official to enter transformed into the domain of spirit-possession in the magic mountain, not as tragedy, commonly understood, which is where the violence in the sacred covenant comes from, but as pure expenditure of the gift element in this covenant along the lines Nietzsche reserved for the mimicry peculiar to the abandon of the Dionysian.

Hence the magic of reversal, built into the magic of the state, redirecting the accursed share, is quintessentially a magic of caricature and literalization; an abrupt gesture not of demystification but of grotesque accentuation of performed hiddenness achieved by a disingenuous insistence on taking things at face-value and materializing them, as in fetishizing a blue liquid with the name of Confusion and manipulating it in relation to the portrait of the father of the law-founding violence on the face of the currency. Not just a photograph, but a palpable photograph . . . all on the body of the mother, thus staging intermittent exposure of the abject with its irascible horny handed powers of pollution as the magic of the state.

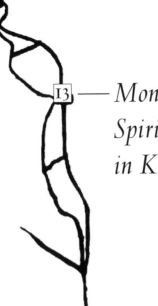

13 — *Money and Spirit Possession in Karl Marx*

His image is everywhere, beginning with the name of the money itself as well as his portrait on many of the denominations. Some bills bear a copy of a monument erected to the victory in the anti-colonial wars. Others display the Liberator in marble astride his horse atop a mountain of dead heaped on the battlefields of the founding violence, ultimately the same mountain that exists in fact and fancy as the enchanted mountain of the spirit queen.

Every monetary transaction thus involves the Liberator.

"The Liberator fell against the dollar today. . . ."

"Twelve Libs for a six-pack."

The meaning dulls with usage, you would think, as the name blurs with the thing it names, a fine example of Nietzsche's notion of metaphor passing into truth as the face on the coin wears away. But on Black Friday (the name tells you all), February 18th 1983, when the first moves in decades towards devaluation were made by the state of the whole of the European Elsewhere to prop up the failing economy, the editor of a weekly magazine was sent to jail for dishonoring the Liberator. His crime had been to print on the cover of the magazine a black cross right across a photograph of a bill. Right across the Liberator's face. Jail!

In the very act of effacing value, defacing magnifies it, drawing out the sacred from the habitual-mundane, illuminating what Nietzsche saw as the shine effaced by usage passing into the illusion of unquestioned factual truth. Defacement puts this habitual operation into reverse; in its hovering between folklore and officialese, no less than between a sad humor and exciting intimations of disaster, the term Black Friday diffuses with the graceful ease of anonymity throughout the realm until it stimulates the forbidden black cross across the face of him whose realm was blackened that Friday that now is legend. Defacement is a strange crime, and one made all the weirder by the question of value it levels both at money and at the state, indeed, at value itself.

"In the long history of attempts to explain the functioning of the economic system," writes Professor Vickers in his book on the theory of money published in 1959, "no problem has enjoyed more diversity of interpretation than that of the theory of money." He notes with irritation that "the problem of money has been the hunting ground of charlatans and cranks." But let us not be too irritated. Let us instead ponder why money provides such a hunting ground and whether, in fact, it is possible not to be a crank or a charlatan on this ground. Indeed it is curious how unproblematic and taken for granted money is, when, after all, it is called upon to do truly miraculous things. Karl Marx began his analysis of money quoting Gladstone to the effect that even love has not turned more men into fools than has meditation upon the nature of money. Not money, mind you, but meditation upon money.

And so bedeviled is Marx with circulation — with the importance for value of circulation — that he too seems smitten with this same foolishness, bowled over by the literalness of money — with its rounded shape as coinage! He begins his discussion of coins and symbols of value by noting "that money takes the shape of coin, springs from its function as the circulating medium."

He captures this roundedness in quite other ways as well, in roundabout de-literalising ways as with his genius for sarcasm — sarcasm itself being a singular rhetoric of circularity transforming value — when he writes that "gold circulates because it has value, whereas paper [money] has value because it circulates."

Now for a long time money has served two functions simultaneously, being both a measure of value and a mediator of exchange in the massive wheel of circulation called the economy. That money can do this is thanks to amazing and deep-seated changes that occurred in the nature of society, changes that allowed for an intricate translation back and forth between concrete particularity and abstract universalism. Money is the sum and measure of this extraordinary cultural achievement.

Another way of saying this is to note that it is because most everything, especially human labor, has become a commodity for purchase on the market, that money serves as both the measure and mediator of otherwise dissimilar things. From an infinitude of diversity — oil out, cars, ammo, and videos in — money speaks with a single voice, the common measure of all. This alone should grant it respect bordering on the sacred. Indeed, money, says Karl Marx, serves in capitalism as the "universal equivalent of value" and value is congealed labor-power.

Astride the mountain of dead riveting the state of the whole to the earth's fiery core, the Liberator testifies to this. For he is truly the Universal whose victorious emergence from the death-space founding the state endorses value and in whose image money not only facilitates the exchange of difference, but opens up Marx to other readings — readings wherein money is the bearer of congealed spiritual labor-power orchestrated by the state of the whole which, after all, not only designs, prints, mints, regulates, and vouchsafes money like God does man in His own image, continuing that magnificent operation of salvation of the sacred remains begun in 1842, but is the very Godhead itself, the state as repository of redemption no less than the promise of credit on which the circulation of coins and notes, like the angels and the wandering souls of purgatory, depend.

Astride the mountain of dead carved in the rumpled mass of granite the Liberator testifies to this.

But we know he is not alone. We know to which other realm, *her* realm, the spirits of these dead escape from their immobilization in granite. The universal equivalent of value turns out to be a split thing split between the statue in every public square, and the lengthening shadow she casts across the faces in the square with the setting of the sun.

The question then arises as to what constitutes the authority that stamped as effigy on metal or paper makes it money. "'Tis the public authority upon the metal that makes it money," notes Nicholas Barbon in his "Discourse Concerning New Money . . . " (in answer to

Mr. Locke), published in London in 1696 and cited by Marx in 1876. Compare with President Bill Clinton, March 8th, 1994: "Trust is the coin of the realm."

Eminently a social product, this authority in the money that makes it money is the quintessence of circularity bound to the fiction that the state of the whole can and will pay up on its money which is advanced as promissory note to the citizenry and, indeed, to the world at large. Of course the state could never pay up if all the citizens wanted to cash in their money for "real" value and it would be rare to find a citizen who actually considered such a possibility nevertheless. The crucial thing is that circulation is sustained because in the ultimate instance—which must never come—there can be recourse to *the hoard.*

The hoard must lie locked outside of circulation in some preeminently exterior and massively secured location continuously replenished with fantasies of power and abundance by those circulating its promissory notes across shop counters and in the streets as much as by those faxing their millions across the screens of the world's financial institutions. Were we to stop and ask the question as to whether Fort Knox—like a castle in a fairy story, surrounded by fearsome military bases and training schools—really had sufficient gold to back all those U.S. dollars, we would soon change the question to ask questions about secrecy and mysticism: whether the Fort's function in maintaining the value of money and therewith the world monetary system had in fact everything to do with its mythic expression of, first, exteriority to circulation and, second, the fairy-tale force of gold and, third, the military prowess evidenced in protecting the hoard.

Like the Tomb of the Unknown Soldier glittering in its dark emptiness, Fort Knox was a fundamentally tabooed space filled with wild imagining, and it is tribute to the postmodern age in which I write that not even the concrete particularity of gold nor that of Fort Knox are now required to give presence and body to the abstract universal which money mediates across the globe. But the idea and the necessity for the idea live on—as with the World Bank and the institutions created at Bretton Woods which, precisely because they themselves lie external to the laws of circulation and the free market, are able to dictate the terms of misery to untold millions of people to the refrain of free competition and the sacred laws of the market. "They are not accountable," says Susan George, who goes on to point out that this exteriority has allowed the bank not only to drive global markets but make huge profits as well. "We are not sure what this system is called," she writes with Fabrizio Sabelli, "but it is not capitalism." If anything it's like the medieval Church.

Equally crucial to "the public authority upon the metal that makes it money" is the banal fact that its circulation, which is its life-force, depends on the citizens of each and every nation-state agreeing to agree on money's value and money's function. To the fiction of the glistening hoard external to the system of circulation, we have to add this other sort of fiction, this agreement to agree, internal and habitual, we could say, to circulation itself.

In which case it is not surprising that money, token and measure of value, is itself thick with the innerness of a troubled and self-inquisitorial soul with regards to its own value and with regards to the relation between reality and fiction. Money — if you like — is pre-modern in that while strange powers stem from its belonging to a system of circulation, those powers seem to emanate not from the *system*, if that's the word, of circulation, but from the physical substance of money "itself" and this is probably the main reason why there are such strict laws against currency defacement — as evidenced by Adam Smith's concern with the real value of money. Barely able to stem his petulance (you can almost see him thumping the table), he asserts that " in every country in the world, I believe, the avarice and injustice of princes and sovereign states, abusing the confidence of their subjects, have by degrees diminished the real quantity of metal, which had originally been contained in their coins."

Here with the concern as to the inner substance of value we encounter the presence of the sovereign — not just his presence, mind you, but his presence as avarice and injustice. President Clinton only got half of it when he said trust is the coin of the realm. In any event value as a presence intimating something hard and physical, like a metal, fuses with the auratic immanence of princely being and in doing so the mystery of money — meditation upon which makes more men fools than even love does — evokes masking, force, and fraud, as when Smith goes on to observe that with currency manipulation by the prince, appearance is able to triumph over reality such that the world of real value and, equally important, reliable measurement of that value, is subject to a law of entropy, to continuous loss. No matter how much the wealth of nations may expand, the prince's mysterious manipulations threaten decline due to his debasing (but never, mind you, defacing) the currency. Like the world's energy, the world's value is being spent by the prince jerking off instead of bowing to what history holds in store in the form of bourgeois dictates of scarcity and rational choice — although what's really at issue here is not the prince so much as the bourgeois *resentiment* and fear of the possibility of a radically different type of economic science, undreamt of by our coiner of the invisible hand, as to do not with the means-ends logic of scarcity or production, but with spending and masking.

For the prince is indeed a great masker and spender. "By means of those operations," writes Smith, "the princes and sovereign states which performed them were enabled in appearance to pay their debts and to fulfill their engagements with a smaller quantity of silver than would otherwise have been requisite."

And if the state of the whole must always be personified, as by the prince, then with equal justice — for here we speak of justice, and therefore of law, as much as of money, value, and appearance — then with equal justice the prince will be monumentalised not just on the money but with money overflowing and spilling forth, the hoard let loose as act of sacral discharge tied to the death of the prince. Always to the death.

Isabel S. Alderson has left us a description of the Liberator's glorious (second) burial when his (im)mortal remains were paraded through the streets of the capital in 1842. Her father knew the Liberator. Her memoir appeared in 1928 in the Journal of the National History Archive. Even in this scholarly journal the very first sentence has to "presence" the dead man in an exquisite balancing act between sacred and profane — and does so not through the personal, nostalgic, memoir of persons, for instance via her father, but instead by shedding the person for the personage and the personage for the monument of the Liberator set astride his tomb in the Cathedral in the capital, a monument of "the purest white marble." We access the intangibility of spirit through the solidity of the monument.

On each side of the Liberator sits a figure.

On one side is the figure of abundance scattering coins.

On the other is the figure of justice, blindfolded, holding her scales.

Here, then, in the purest white marble we see *the scene of money*, money being scattered, scattering, *derramando*, which also means money spilling, money overflowing, money leaking, money discharging, money hemorrhaging . . . by the side of the Liberator by the side of Law astride his sacred bones in the Cathedral.

Money, says Karl Marx, serves in capitalism as the universal equivalent of value, and value is congealed labor power.

But what is this value, this congealed labor-power?

At times you can read Marx and the other great economists of his era (when philosophers of that changing world worried about such things as "value") as if they were searching for the lodestone, the "Fort Knox" of value, and, determined that this quintessence resides in "labor."

But the value of labor?

Well, that resides in . . . the value of the commodities required to reproduce labor!

Once more the circle, the Great Wheel rumbling, and again the figure of the prince intervenes to remind us that "labor" is not only a power like horse-power or a natural substance to be bought and sold like gasoline but also and always a matter of command and submission, a matter of control over the bodily and creative power of another human being — albeit effected not through politics per se, not through slavery or serfdom or family, but through "freedom of the market," the freedom that was fought for in the founding violence against the mercantilism of the colonial power so as to open up trade worldwide and establish the civil rights of a citizenry in place of castes and slavery. It was one of the intellectual triumphs of Marxism to have investigated how the person was translated into the worker and how the worker was translated by market culture into a reified object of labor and how therefore command over persons is effected through the anonymity of market mechanisms, how cruelty and exploitation and all manner of degradations and glory were effected through the language of numbers, efficiency, and substances. But what seem to have often been lost from sight in tracing this move from the literality of personhood to the abstraction of number and thinghood are both the original impulse to investigate the conditions for human freedom and the recognition that the reified notion of "labor" was precisely a mechanism for control over persons and bodies.

As Adam Smith puts it — and it is largely from Smith, Petty, and Ricardo that Marx takes the "labor theory of value" — as Smith puts it, the value of any commodity is equal to the quantity of labor which it enables the owner of that commodity to purchase or command. The word *command* here alerts us to the willful nature of the transactions implicated in the *labor theory of value*. We are used to Smith reading the bourgeois present by imposing it onto the history of the world and then reading that present as a consequence, and here, with labor we find the originary point for just such a reading. Smith puts it like this. "Labor was the first price, the original purchase-money that was paid for all things. It was not by gold or silver, but by labor, that all the wealth of the world was originally purchased; and its value, to those who possess it, and who want to exchange it for some new productions, is precisely equal to the quantity of labor which it can enable them to purchase or command."

Value, therefore, even and especially in the state of freedom created by the self-regulating market, is ultimately command over labor by means of command over people as things. The problem of the particular in relation to the abstract reasserts itself in the equation of value and this is why the prince, he who commands, must always figure in value, all the more so when he stands behind it, as on the face of the currency.

But then how is it that in the state of freedom with all things paid for at a fair price where slavery has been abolished and so many have died for freedoms in the founding violence for national sovereignty and republican government, how is it then that labor can be made to create a surplus? By what mysterious alchemy does labor, without the force that existed in colonial times, yield more value at the end of the day than what there was at the beginning when, following the rule of the market, it is paid its market price?

Here unavoidably we come to Marx's discussion of money in relation to the weird architecture and dynamism of the commodity-form — an architecture he sees through the lens of Hegel's abiding concern with value as lying in the relation between the concrete particular thing and the universal — Hegel's question being how to privilege the concreteness but also the universality that allows difference to be discerned and hence serve as a basis for comparison and valuation.

In his *Elements of the Philosophy of Right,* for instance, Hegel runs money through this ontological-historical mill where he writes: "The value of a thing can vary greatly in relation to need; but if one wishes to express not the specific nature of its value but its value in the abstract, this is expressed as money. Money can represent anything, but since it does not depict the need itself but is only a sign in place of it, it is itself governed in turn by the specific value which it expresses in the abstract."

In this weird symbolic and quintessentially circular power of money mediating the concrete with the abstract, then, lies the exquisite problem of rhetoric mediating words with things, abstract universals with concrete particulars and, most especially, metaphoricity with literality — to such effect that only the state monument can serve to arrest the interaction in the white purity of its marble; the father accompanied by the hemorrhaging of money, to one side, justice on the other, this blind justice that requires from the father both the force of arms and the mystique of death. This reminds us that while indeed money not only sums up the ineffably complex problem of representation, zig-zagging back and forth between the (illusion of the) concrete and the (artefactuality of the) abstract, it does so thanks to a central authority outside of money itself — namely the state, which, however, is itself significant for its always being beyond…being itself something not just elusive but generative of masking and interiority and defined by such. Like money, the state is thick with soulstuff.

It is the most important commodity of all, namely labor-power, that provides the illustration, if not solution, to the riddle of surplus value. The possessor of this commodity sells it to the employer as abstract and universal labor-power whose worth is what Marx (following Adam Smith and Aristotle) calls "exchange value." But like any commodity, this labor-power is consumed by the purchaser — i.e., the person who comes to "possess" it — not as an abstract exchange-value but as a particular and concrete use-value. This exchange from the general abstract to the concrete particular is thus the first step in the circuit, the first step into the current mediated by currency.

The purchaser of labor-power then deploys his or her new possession in its carnal embodied mode as concrete and particular use-value to create "exchange value" (i.e., abstract and universal labor-power) in the form of commodities that are to be sold, thus more or less closing the circuit, the alchemical trick being that with all the rules of market free-dom scrupulously observed, it is this transfer in status between use and exchange value that creates surplus value. In summary, the dynam-ic architecture of the commodity-form is precisely this circuit effected by the exchange of selling and buying in which abstract value is trans-formed into carnal mode so as to fortify abstract value. A commodity is a process-sensitive hybridinal composite of use and exchange value, of concretion and abstraction, whose separate parts are now joined, now separated, now rejoined, in the great circuit mediated by money of buy-ing and selling, possessing and dispossessing, separating, exchang-ing, rejoining. and creating surplus.

The abiding point of this amazing yet everyday phenomenon is its ability to swell in value as a result of its *incarnating abstraction*, to traverse the circuitous route from abstraction to concrete particularity and *return with more*—just as the person possessed by a spirit of the dead returns with more, with the magical power to set aright the trials and tribulations of life's journey itself.

Whether or not we agree with Marx is not as important as tracing the importance of circulation-and-metamorphosis in his argument. For in following the circle of his reasoning we become sensitized to the properties thereof and can then do our own wheeling and dealing, mindful of the power that circulation exercised over fledgling economic science. It obsessed mercantilist theory, for instance, and gave rise to vivid, if varied, images, being compared with blood by Hobbes and by writers before him in the sixteenth century, to the soul by others, while Bacon declared "money is like Muck, not good except it be spread."

The curious thing is that Marx, too, is obsessed by circulation. His writing swarms with biologistic and magical allusions in the effort to render justice to what he sees as the strange powers of circulation. He never lets us forget that "the economy" is a social process of restless circulatory activity of interacting qualities and forces whose engagement means change and newness. His prose is splattered throughout with reference to crystals forming out of liquids, liquids passing back into crystals, metamorphoses, social metabolism, the dramatic encounter of life and death, and even alchemy. What emerges as crucial is that the value-creating function of labor as measured and mediated by money is:

■ Totally dependent on circulation, and that
■ Circulation entails transformation,
■ Most especially the transformation spiraling back and forth between the concrete particularity of any given labor and the embodiment of that labor as abstract and universal in the commodity that that labor has helped fashion, and,
■ It is this last feature, so commonplace and yet so mysterious, of a back and forth transfer incarnating abstraction that money mediates and from which value is created.

Now, consider spirit possession, the performance of embodiment and disembodiment—especially the theater embodying the spirit-force of a sexually bifurcated Universal Idea flowing through a conglomeration of spirits bound to a tenuously centralized hierarchy crowned by the aura of the Liberator "shadowed" by the spirit queen.

■ A crucial feature of this theater of spirit-possession is that the circulation of spirits of the dead through live human bodies is a movement parallel to the circulation of the ghostly magic of the Nation-State through the "body" of the society — as when the President of the Republic invokes as part of the daily round of statecraft the "spirit" of the Liberator, and Ofelia, the healer on the spirit queen's mountain, in her turn invokes the spirit too, but as "literal fact." Here everything hinges on the necessity and impossibility of collapsing spirit into literal fact.

■ Thus spirit possession on the magic mountain on the margins of the profane world resurrects as "literal fact" the haunting quality of metaphor buried in the abject mix of absurdity and fear constituting the kitsch-prowess of the self-representation of the state of the whole. The mountain of the spirit queen is the fount of spiritual labor which discharges the surplus consumed by the state of the whole which includes amongst its authorizations that of endorsing the currency and the current of the Liberator himself.

So much for the value-creating function of labor. What Ofelia calls "my work." No wonder if money stands at the center of this it has been called the hunting ground of cranks and charlatans. Let us try to slow this dizzying circuit a little by asking Marx about the source of value that money mediates and measures and let us try to follow his reasoning that value lies not in a *source* nor in *exchange* per se, but instead in the *metamorphosis* of the object or service exchanged — that value lies in *transformation*.

This metamorphosis has a bewilderingly magical nature to it. In fact Marx refers to the process that occurs when a commodity is exchanged for money and the money used to purchase another commodity as *alchemical*. And this is one of his favorite metaphors; circulation and subsequent metamorphoses occur as though inside what he calls an "alchemistical retort." (A retort is a glass flask into which you can place chemicals and then apply heat. In the case of the alchemists it refers to the mixing of chemicals with a base metal such as lead so as to convert that metal into a precious metal such as gold.)

As we shall see, his entire theory relies heavily for its exposition on magical allusion organized through a series of cascading tableaus. Reading Marx with this in mind you see that the celebrated "fetishism of commodities" concept is merely the tip of the spiritual iceberg. Not even Marx at his sarcastic best can escape the mysteries that enshroud money as that hunting ground for cranks and charlatans. To the contrary, his text seems to welcome the mysteries and gleefully embrace them in that instant before they crush him. He does not demystify so much as play mystery off against mystery, magic against magic in the Karl Marx *son et lumiere* spectacular, and his own theory is of necessity complicit with the alchemy it appears to scoff at.

Nowhere is his exposition more deeply complicit than in the importance he gives to the magic of the dead and to embodiment of spirit as vital to both the architecture and circulation of the commodity-form. Indeed, he is no less dramatic than a spirit medium, escorting us into the seance of capitalist circulation of metamorphosing powers. This is a language of religious sacrifice in which labor is holy fire. That is strange enough. But why does death figure so much? Why is it necessary for value to be so continuously at work on the dead?

"Living labor must seize upon these things [machinery, iron, wood, and yarn]," writes Marx, "and rouse them from their death-sleep, change them from mere possible use-values into real and effective ones. Bathed in the fire of labor, appropriated as part and parcel of labor's organism, and, as it were, made alive for the performance of their functions in the process, as elementary constituents of new use-values, of new products . . .

"By turning his money into commodities that serve as the material elements of a new product, and as factors in the labor-process, by incorporating living labor with their dead substance, the capitalist at the same time converts value, i.e., past, materialized, and dead labor into capital, into value big with value, a live monster that is fruitful and multiplies."

Now whatever death's exact function in the alchemistical retort of modern capitalist circulation that converts base metal into precious metals, Marx understands this to be swirling with contradiction because only by having opposites interact in exchange in circulation can the magic of alchemy fire off its extraordinary metamorphoses. Alchemy, we might say, is the applied science of death-and-contradiction in the laboratory of modernity.

The first metamorphosis occurring in the alchemical retort is when the commodity is sold for money. Interacting and necessarily completing this is the second metamorphosis, when the money is used to purchase another commodity. That this process is modeled on a dramatic performance, Marx leaves no doubt. "The complete metamorphosis of a commodity," he writes, "implies four extremes, and three dramatis personae," a performance in which the commodity-form (1) appears, (2) is then stripped down, and (3) finally returns to itself but now (4) swollen with augmented value; hence C—M—C'. To do justice to this, Marx cannot avoid a magical language as well as a theatrical one, a language of mysterious appearances and disappearances, of stripping away, of things passing into other things, and of crystallization and liquefaction. "So, too, the money appears in the first phase [of circulation] as a solid crystal of value," he writes, "a crystal into which the commodity eagerly solidifies." But as he also wrote, along with his friend the young Frederick Engels in a famous manifesto in 1848, with modern capitalism, "all that is solid melts into air."

We might want to think of circulation as organic and fluid, and there is of course good reason for that. But circulation of the alchemical type analyzed here moves to a different rhythm, a staggered sort of thing more or less blindly shouldering its way through a series of shocks and epileptic impulses made out of composing and decomposing ensembles in tensed encounter, negotiated comings-together, couplings, transfers, and disengagements.

These circuits of staggering syncopation are indeed miraculous because they achieve their closure, ephemeral as it is, in the fiery diffuseness of chronic crisis in which the exception is the rule. Here then is the unimaginable state of permanent crisis, the magical scene of philosophy no less than of everyday life in our alchemical times, and if what should be an intimate connection (as between selling and buying — could there be a greater intimacy?) is too prolonged, thus blocking the metamorphoses from interacting, then, as Marx engagingly puts it, the oneness of the entire process asserts itself by producing a crisis — as happens constantly in what economists call "the business cycle." Then the antitheses and contradictions immanent in commodities that unite the metamorphosing interactions in circulation diverge to follow their own modes of motion.

Is it possible that the theater of spirit possession is not merely a privileged coupling of body with spirit but is, above all, this miraculous theater of the stammering syncopation of the ever-present crisis in circulation, exploiting the never-ending crisis of embodiment of the particular in the universal, thus steadying the state of the whole even as it plunges into the next shuddering crisis of sovereignty that is, in fact, sovereignty itself?

And if it is the role of the body to be thick here, thick with soul and performed innerness, like the state itself, this human body which must through *velaciones* be diligently purified in silence by the shrines on the magic mountain so as to receive spirit in glorious enactments of embodiedness, this body so long condemned to the taboo-world of the ambiguously unclean, let us not forget that it is spirit possession which enables us to read differently, to read Marx and therefore capitalism differently, to become that much more sensitive to the alchemical play of death-in-contradiction. Let us not forget, furthermore, that such an alchemical reading as the applied science of contradiction in the laboratory of modernity is itself both circular and staggered, fitfully and finally achieving its starting point in the looping intercourse between taboo and transgression where the crisis-riddled nature of sovereignty passes through the spirit queen.

Here at the end of our circle appears once more not only the underside of stately prowess in the figure of the woman that is the spirit queen, but the figure of defacement as with the man gaoled for defacing the Liberator's face on the face of the currency. For is it not in keeping with a certain disposition towards death and negation that *defacement* should bring forth sacred investitures otherwise lost in the everydayness of things, one route leading to jail, the other to her mountain? Through desecration and sacrilege, defacement creates value, an inspired sickness of the soul testifying to and honoring the magical power of taboo in which many forms of alchemy lie latent and not only the ones that will take you to jail.

Listen!

A man is being questioned about the Liberator, a man known for his love of singing at wakes. Someone wants to know what the people are thinking about the Liberator in this sunny Elsewhere and what he says will make its way into an ethnographic type of book published by the press of the University of the Liberator in the capital for the bicentenary of the birth of the Liberator. Let us at once note that this man is an arch-defacer. He says:

"At a wake or on an altar, the first thing you'll come across is a portrait of the Liberator. In a person's home, also, the first thing you'll come across is a portrait of the Liberator. It's always there. He's not just a person who made a history, but someone who did something great. And you have to request something! This is our system and also of foreigners, because if you're not with the Liberator you're not going to get mobilized. One makes a petition to him so as to get something. To begin with, the system of mobilization is the money, so that when you need to overcome a problem, take hold of the palpable photograph of the Liberator, up to a large bill and if you have a personal problem or someone in your family is in prison, take hold of the portrait of the Liberator, a glass of water, light a candle, and make a petition with devotion. Your problem will be solved.

"It's as if it was really the image of the Liberator that did it."

"Faith is necessary. Always.

In any event, be aware or even beware you ethnographers and you ethnographised of those asking questions for the Liberator's bicentenary, feeding the magic of currency into the current—into the great cycle of stuttering translation of meaning and force siphoning upward through the class and race hierarchy, alchemically converting the literal into the metaphoric, there to descend to the masses to be recirculated once again "bathed in the fires of labor . . ."

Above all beware of forgeries. For forgers of the currency abound, their patient hands and sharp eyes capable of (dis)simulating every detail — as if the seed disseminated by his death in the all-alike memory fragments of currency insists on proliferation and mad escapades of exuberant expenditure—not only in the realm of copying through spirit-possession, but also in the copying undertaken in the artesanal factories of the underworld in rites of secrecy and exactitude as prelude to entering the legal circuits of exchange.

So it befalls the state of the whole to take charge here and designate how much of this stuff to print and circulate and what shape, color, size, and pictures it should have. All this the defacing man being asked questions intuits through his awareness of the magic of money, that something is at stake in this official picture circulating from hand to hand like the souls of the dead scattered across the land passing through the unclean bodies of the living in flurries of fear and desire. The man interrupts the circuit for a moment and takes the portrait of the Liberator to task.

And this man is everywhere.

"Part Detective, Part-Diviner," is how Paul Levy of Merril Lynch was described on page one of *The Wall Street Journal*, January 2nd, 1987, after his fifteenth or so trip here from New York City to ascertain the health of the Liberator. The *Journal* article set off a storm of protest here because fact-gathering economists, especially from organs such as Merril Lynch, are not meant to be detectives (who investigate obscured crimes) and certainly not diviners (who use magic to ascertain the occult), even though that is what the vagaries of the economy and the secrets of state brought out from Mr. Levy's otherwise unremarkable demeanor as an economist working for the world's super rich.

For the *Journal* packs a lot of punch here and people are sensitive to the slightest hint of ridicule concerning matters of sovereignty as involved in who is allowed to speak on such a delicate matter as "the economy." Indeed their very indignation at the notion of divination in this question of the currency testifies to the sanctity with which they hold both the nation and its money.

And this man is everywhere.

The points to dwell on are first the mysterious threads that combine secrecy with the sacred, and second that the entity we fondly unify as the state *appears* to keep certain information secret. Such information includes not merely policies, as whether to devalue or not and by what amount, but also seemingly hard facts accomplished like oil production. Facts such as these amount to secrets of state and cannot be revealed or, if they are, are likely to be false in order to affect the market. Then there are other secrets such as the problem of the multinational firms with their hundred and one ways of defining and hiding figures behind Nation-States like cards in a shell-game, not to mention the cavalier assumptions made as to peasant production and consumption, and of course the wild guesses made as to the so-called "service sector," amounting to some forty percent of the GNP! And this is just the beginning.

In other words, the basis of national accounting (modeled, of course, on systems devised and imported from Paris), including major indices such as the GNP, is phony.

But even to call something phony is to instill a false sense of security and hence profoundly underestimate the massive degree of uncertainy, deception, bluff, and ignorance on which such gargantuan enterprises as the ship of state rest.

It's not just that these major economic indicators are based in part on inspired and not so inspired guess-work, and in part on deliberate lies. More important still is the enormously revealing fact that simply because they bear the imprimatur of the modern state, such figures are accorded a knock-around practical status they in no way deserve —and more important than secrecy and deliberate deceit in this regard, which at least gesture towards the familiar fantasy of a reassuringly real and motivated order of somebody or some thing, after all, conspiring behind the facade, far more important than this is the truly sacred secrecy achieved through either the denial of secrecy or, stronger still, the claim that there is secrecy when, in fact, the real official secret is that there is none. With this latter masterful stroke, the performance of hidden innerness is called into play and the state of the whole assured sublime status.

All this the defacing man being asked questions naturally intuits. . . .

Mr. Levy's task according to *The Wall Street Journal* involved analyzing political trends "in nations [unlike the United States, of course] in which politics is played out largely in the shadows, affecting economic growth in ways which can only be surmised." We now know from whose abject realm these shadows reach, this treacherous, powerful, realm of hers into which the detective-diviner makes his way, now as much an anthropologist as diviner. In a typical three-day visit to the capital of this sunny land he is busy interviewing informants; people who run foreign-exchange agencies, edit economic reviews, run banks, and so forth. Mr Levy has hunches about their hunches. This is the key thing.

Mr. Prunhuber for instance, who runs a small economic newsletter and who migrated here from New York City in 1921 drops "an interesting tidbit": that the country has, *he thinks*, exhausted its reserves of its currency, the Liberator, and if that is true, Mr. Levy *thinks*, the government will have to print more money to finance its budget and that will stoke inflation. Mr. Levy makes notes on his pad. Over an expensive lunch with an important agri-businessman, Mr. Levy hears that the government is not reciprocating with the business community and that his host is asking relatives in other countries how they cope with inflation. Mr. Levy concludes that the private sector is pessimistic and that could be a serious impediment for economic growth. Mood is everything. A senior economist in the central bank tells him that the drain on the country's reserves of U.S. dollars is bigger than expected, and that some of these dollars are going to support the Liberator in foreign-exchange markets. Mr. Levy is startled. The situation is worse than he thought. The Liberator would be even weaker without central bank intervention. "Now politics is a more important variable to
take into account," he concludes. "These people are living in a fools' paradise."

All this the defacing man being asked questions naturally intuits.

And this man is everywhere.

And so is she.

14 — Art Adrift in the Passing Crowd Floating Wave-Like on a Freeway

What is this strange force roaming the public space in the image of the father seeking right of passage through memory made luminous by his shadowy consort, the spirit queen, enigmatically smiling in her mountain with the spirits of the dead? What is this strange force that casts public space as so many replicas of her enchanted mountain, selecting strategic points for the signature of the Liberator for the completion of sacred signs?

THOSE WHO ABANDON ALL TO SERVE THE FATHERLAND LOSE NOTHING & WILL BECOME ONE WITH THE SAINTS

What is the status of this state graffiti hovering between the absurd and the horrific, inching towards sanctity? Note its diffusion into the tiniest particles of the Nation-State such as this settlement of three or four huts. Note also the aura specific of stately presence, the signs of paranoia — their signs of fear that make you fear. Along the walls of the police station are sacks of sand against which lounge three police with black pistols no less conspicuous than their machine gun. They are guarding one of the road-barriers found throughout this democratic Elsewhere where gas is dirt cheap and cars abound. Oil out; guns, ammo, videos, and cars in.

Once Mission stopped at one of these road-barriers. There were two men in uniform and one in plain clothes (as expression has it), sitting in their little temple "watching" the traffic. The one in plain clothes was of slight build and held a silver pistol in his crotch pointed towards the traffic, but hidden below the window sill. What did he think was going to happen?

ARE NOT THESE BARRIERS THE SHRINES AND MAGIC GATEWAYS OF THE STATE ITSELF?

As you pass through in your car at a snail's pace, coiling like a spring, awaiting the policeman, arm at the ready, to nod you on, does not your all too studied casualness, your studied disconcern, resemble the zombie-facies of the entranced, spread-eagled in front of a *portal* on the spirit-queen's mountain? Do you not for ever so prolonged a brief moment of tensedness become possessed by the spirit — the spirit of the state? We would do well to remember that

ONE IMPRUDENT STEP COULD BURY US FOREVER

Remembering that Arnold Van Gennep's first example of rites of passage was the passage across territorial borders, as though this *spatial* passage was the elementary and *ur*-form of ritual, we might want to think more about the mystery-making and theatrical quality of *everyday* state rituals — not only the lavish spectacles establishing the center of power, but the small and everyday rites of passage . . . like that which transpires in passing through the police controlled road barriers that are so abundant. Of course this *rite de passage* is not so much a movement from one social status to another, from youth to adult, for example, as it is a purifying transition from a potentially criminal status — but only until the next time, when the purifying recommences, or so we hope.

The logic is eminently reversible because these barriers can be seen as polluting, not purifying, in that they declare all who pass through them to be suspect and dirty. We remember the man in "plain clothes" seated with his silver pistol out of sight pointed towards the traffic. To pass by this man is not necessarily to be cleansed or relieved of the strange guilt that being a member of a modern state seems to imply. Indeed it is more likely that one feels lucky at having successfully run the gauntlet of a disturbing irrationality and this time, at least, been blessed by the small miracle and allowed through unscathed. Until the next time . . .

To speak of the miraculous in this starkly secular world of concrete pill boxes, sand bags, dark glasses, and bullet-proof vests, is to merely raise, once again, the mystery of the presence of God in modernity, the mystery in other words as to the problematic nature of His death and hence the terrifying possibility that in modernity God has neither ceased to exist, nor continues to exist as God, but instead exists as Dead God equipped therefore with powers far surpassing Live God, blessed as the dead are with the capacity to possess the living, especially by means of the theatrics of the stately everyday.

Occasionally these everyday productions, routinised as they are, have to blow up and achieve the scale of the spectacular so as to maintain the explosive promise of His deadly presence otherwise secured in minute particulars, in the promise lying dormant in the contract the statue makes with the face of the crowd in the public square. As Bataille instructs in his essay on that great needle of stone, the obelisk, taken from ancient Egypt to modern France so as to provide a certain body to the imperial image of state, this promise of deadly presence no less powerful than that of a superseded sun is a force arising from the concreteness of images "that a kind of lucid dream borrows from the realm of the crowd." (And let us not forget that most concrete of images in modernity, concrete itself.)

Sometimes a presence hidden in the shadows of these dreams borrowed from the realm of the crowd is brought to light while, at other times, figures routinely ignored are suddenly highlighted. This brings to mind the gist of Robert Musil's remark many decades past concerning the invisibility and half-life of statues, how they live unnoticed by the passing crowd.

But now we have to further emphasize the passing, the atomized yet flowing nature of this crowd, for this presents a quite new set of circumstances for presencing the power of the dead and their figuration of stately being. For a thinker who once selected delirious excesses of speed in fast automobiles as evocative of *expenditure* as both feeling and philosophy, it is strange that Bataille chose to focus on the center and hence a center-periphery tension, on the public square, its obelisk and its crowd, instead of on the deterritorializing street and highway as traversed by the automobile, registered by the state and driven under state license.

For we cannot be oblivious to the fact that this move from the public square to the freeway is as different a movement of body and thought as it is of image and that the magic of the state is as every much this deterritorialising set of momentums as it is the territorialising erection of the monument "that a kind of lucid dream borrows from the realm of the crowd." And what is incomparable is the nature of the gift that the lucid dream borrows from the crowd so as to effect a transfer of movement between the two — between the stasis and the dispersion no less than between the statue and the crowd — at that undefinable point where the one becomes the other, perhaps at the Tomb of the Unknown Soldier. For although He sits stiff-backed dead coming to life on horseback atop the rumpled granite that is the mountain of dead fallen in those anti-colonial wars and wars within those wars, it is another speed altogether that stirs at the base of that mountain of bodies to flow out as a great river of death through the Arch of Triumph and the Tomb of the Unknown Soldier and then spread as an endless plain of white concrete in its steady monotony of shimmering heat across the field of battle that settled the fate of nations to become the freeway system stretching across them.

Here on the road exists an even more exalted space for the monument in both its routine invisibility and its sudden flares of sacral discharge, especially when threatened with that most loved and feared of all acts — defacement. For if it is defacement that brings out the

sacred quality of stately things, if it requires this force of the negative to externalize the sacred within, then we must also be made aware of the wide range of stately activities whose main purpose for existence lies precisely in their both attracting-and-preventing such defacement so as to maintain, through a type of sacred masturbation, the quasi-religious basis of the modern state.

March, 1988: Pre-fieldwork; Arriving. 6:00 in the morning, tired, surrounded by men talking about money and making more of it, then an anxious silence as queues formed to go through immigration (note the almost familiar, almost animistic, usage here, "into immigration" — as though it's a thing with a mind, etc.). The men put on the Face and herd their families like sheep through the barrier, clutching passports in their hands like talismans endowed with magic by virtue of their transmitting the spermatic economy of the state. The Immigra-tion Officer motions Mission brusquely to one side declaring deadpan he needs a visa. Mission says he's never needed one before. A few other "foreigners" join him penned in this no-man's land between and constitutive of Nation-States where the visa-less live, if it can be called living, shorn of all hope of identity ye who have had to enter here. No way of knowing what's going on. The streams of bodies shuffle through the gateway, grateful for the stamping received. Thuds and whacks fill the air. The percussion without which no rite of passage is possible. Thud. Thud. Whack. Whack. A veritable twenty-one gun salute. The sound of a fist with inky rubber in it hitting paper fills the room, together with the scuffle of feet as each individual smiles gratefully at the faceless stamper as they pass through to the Other Side. Mission appeals to what looks like a superior officer (note the terminology creeping in). The Superior Officer says, No! He doesn't need a visa. Then another one says Yes! He does! Another one, walking replica of the Liberator, says through his mustache and portcullis of gritted teeth, "Wait! Calm yourself *señor!*" The ultimate stylistics of violence. Calm yourself. Mission waits "patiently" like the man from the countryside waiting all his life by the door to the law. Twenty minutes tumble through the sluice-gates of the grey area. Remember:

One imprudent step could bury us forever

Finally he sees the light and adroitly passes over twenty dollars and his "visa" is issued. Two confused German hippies, convinced they'll find justice, refuse to pass into the dank interzone of corruption and remain in the pen shaking their long locks.

Two days later, in the field on the approach to the freeway to the magic mountain in a rented Fiat outside of the city of Valencia. Rachel is driving. It's midday and hot as hell, the glare poking steely fingers into your eyes. They approach a barrier and go through a gateway with a green light where there should be a ticket. Only there is none. Rachel stops on the side of the road and walks back to get a ticket. A cop emerges from a low building with sandbags piled along its side. It looks like pictures of Vietnam during the war, but this is a democracy at peace with itself and the world at large. Another cop lolls along the wall with a shotgun. The first cop is furious. Something heinous is afoot beyond the comprehension of mere mortals. He refuses to listen and demands Rachel's license, takes it across the highway to the Official Building — the one with sandbags, the anal warts of the beleaguered State surrounded by the invisible enemy. They stay in the car. It gets hotter still, the glare slicing the air into strips of screaming nerve tissue. After a few minutes another cop comes and says they're calling on the telephone about her license. "Calling God," Mission tries to joke, it being Easter Thursday and everything Official shut. Ten minutes later the first cop comes back to declare they can't go on because Rachel's license is not international. Then another cop, who seems to be his superior, with close-cropped hair, bullet-proof vest, and wrap-around dark glasses, proceeds to admonish them as if they were criminals or children. You can only drive with an International license. No way around it. You can't move from here. Why did you go through a gateway with a red light on? But there was no red light on, they explained. The fault lies with the freeway personnel; they should either have closed the gateway or had a person there! He does not listen. He cannot listen for he comes from a distant place where the glare is even stronger than here, the place of the special people champing at the bit, stamping talismans held aloft dripping with victory awaiting the stamping of the Liberator's horse, awaiting the Germans to stop shaking their locks and attend to the business of state. He proceeds with his interrogation, searching for secrets of state, eviscerating truth there on a bayonet glinting in the sunlight, admonishing their pronunciation of Spanish. He walks away, telling them to wait. Instead they hit the gas pedal and take off, invoking other gods. An ecstatic moment.

That night, driving out along the dirt road to the magic mountain, they are stopped by police. It is Easter and crowds of pilgrims are expected. The police have formed a barrier at the first shrine, the *portal* of the *indio macho* at the entrance to the sugar mill, lights twinkling. They are persistent with their questions but not hostile. They warm to the theme of the spirit queen whom they hold in respect. They say her mountain is a *monumento nacional*. At Quiballo, further along the road, they say, there is a woman who becomes possessed by a Viking and talks English. The police tell them how dangerous it is in the mountain, but they have swarms of soldiers and police there too. Here then is another zone of danger like the road-barriers with sand-bagged watch-houses. Only here the guardians have translated the spirit queen into a "*monumento nacional*" in a move that both registers and erases her importance. Strange to have a "*monumento nacional*" aswarm with danger, ringed by police. How would the author of *The Golden Bough* have located this?

Conquistador: Freeways and Modernity; true or not, one of the first things your hear about dictators and what seems synonymous with them is their enthusiasm for moving people, with speed, flow, bodies in flight along a stretch of time from the glorious ruins of the Parthenon to the camp at Auschwitz. There is the necessary spectacle of the Center. That is true. But there is this other, this fabulous counter-movement, as well, the Roman Emperors' magnificent roads over barbarian Europe, the *autobahn* and the people's car, the little Volks-Wagen, alongside Mussolini enriching the political vocabulary of the twentieth century by having fancy trains *run on time*, the US government inspired by the greatest stateworks in the history of mankind, the Great Wall of China, into building the massive interstate highways from coast to coast in case of totalitarian invasion, inaugurating at the same time on the Presidential Seal and the dollar itself

In God We Trust

Are not these massive *autobahn* from Long Island to Big Sur the true monuments of modernity, the equivalent of the pyramids and obelisks in ancient Egypt—only a good deal more tied into the cult of the dead, as well as having a vital interactive art-work component? And even as we carouse and cruise the monument of the modern eating up the miles we must ponder why circulation or "transport" (the term used for spirit possession at the magic mountain,) is such a big player in the imagery of the leader.

No matter how fondly our feelings may veer towards the freedom of flight when we cruise and carouse the freeway, we have to admit there is something tenacious about the link between such flight and the state, between cars and policing. In the U.S., cradle of freedom and mobility (generally equated), the driver's license has for decades served as a de facto state identity card, something that would be otherwise shunned in that country as smacking of dictatorship.

The use of the car for social control is perhaps even more marked when a society is on the verge of the big leap forward into car and truck transport — as was this sunny Elsewhere in the 1950s, riding high on the hog of oil exports.

In 1939 there were almost 18,000 registered cars.

Twenty years later, 9,000 cars were being assembled per year.

Four years later, in 1963, this had almost doubled, and by 1973 some 66,000 cars were being assembled per year (as against a mere 21,000 in the neighboring republic of Costaguana with no oil and more than double the population).

By 1982 some 155,000 were being produced. And what meaning these cars had! — gas guzzling American Chevies and Fords like the great white *Conquistador* sweeping across the land in a blaze of sleek macho power, most everything automatic. All that was needed was bulletproof-vested policing for the whole package to come together.

The expression *chevere* that came to signify "wonderful" was in fact derived from the Chevie. Mission used to hear it in the seventies imported into poor Costaguana along with saint José Gregorio on the lips of cane cutters who'd slipped across the border into the Elsewhere. They of course could only dream of ever possessing an automobile. But at least they'd gotten the word and everything around could be thus verbally anointed and given glowing status, scrutinized until it yielded its full flush of splendour as the magic word erupted from its vehicular form. *Chevere.* The word expanded our universe.

Cayagua Beach: when they arrived they were the only people there except for the López family who own a kiosk on the sand and have been here for thirty-six years. That first day Mission was in a trance, lost in the beauty, the heat, and the solitude. They ate biscuits and tomatoes and bought ice cold beer from Señor López. Their two children, aged three and one, had never seen the ocean before. The sunset brought cool relief after the heat of the day and the tension of driving down the narrow road twisting back and forth along the mountain sides. Someone claimed the road was built as an escape route for the president who ruled the country for close to thirty years from the beginning of the century, leading from his haciendas and military bases to this coast, once the economic center of the colony, exporting cacao from slave plantations, now isolated except for the thin ribbon of the avalanche-prone road. The sun set into a flood of pinks, mauves, and deep crimson out beyond the western point of the curving beach. The moon hung for a moment over the cliffs as a thin crescent with the barest hint of a sphere. They hung their hammocks between coconut trees on the sand. The stars burnt in the sky.

The first car came at 11:00 P.M. Then more, driving onto the area between the beach and the forest. They made fires over which they poured gasoline. They had to have fire. In the morning they emerged from low slung American Fords and Chevies, paunchy men in boxer shorts and women in bikinis with bandannas around their hair, like the beer ads on the tv that was on at the López kiosk transmitting the Miss Universe competition to an attentive crowd. Some of the cars got stuck in the sand. It was surprising how their drivers believed their vehicles could, and should, go anywhere they wanted. In the afternoon four-wheel drive Toyotas and Range-Rovers, upper-middle-class cars, eight lights mounted on their roofs, close cousins to the Ford Broncos favored by death squads in El Salvador and Colombia, came down, directly onto the soft sand of the beach proper. A large red Range Rover came tearing along close to the waterline four feet from where the children were playing. In the afternoon the other cars left and the four-wheel drive cars started to race one another, three at a time, along the length of the beach as the tide rose and the sun set, crimson, out beyond the cliffs.

One car got stuck and a second, trying to pull it out, got stuck too. Then the first got free but a third one got stuck trying to extract the second. Night fell. You could see them digging with a shovel, the girls sitting in the cars, motors screaming, lights streaming onto the beach as they all settled deeper into the ever-softer sand. Now and again one of these cars, still free or newly freed, would roar into the dark to get more cable for towing from the nearby village of dark-skinned descendants of the slaves who had worked the cacao plantations. A phosphorescent trail of glittering light wove its way through the coconut trees as they sped through.

There were five cars altogether. The free ones formed an arc around the trapped ones. The men would light cigarettes and shovel more, sweating in their bright swimming costumes, red, blue, and yellow, as the tide rose. The beach was now a battlefield. For half a mile, its full length, there were the furrows made by the speeding cars. Then there were the great holes the men were digging to free their cars, while the spinning wheels made others. It was an unpremeditated ritual dedicated to the forces of modernity and, watching this mixture of panic and beauty, danger and destruction, it was impossible not to think of the other side of this coastal range, of that magical mountain of the dead as the motors screamed into the lonely night, the sand billowed, and the water surged inch by inch to lap at the magical machinery of transportation.

Of course this was a complicated ritual in that it was only partially, consciously designed, and then it had backfired so as to become truly sacred. Incorporating ancient elements of game and speed with tv beer ads and beauty queens, together with the complex of powerful emotions embodied in cars, they had chosen this paradise as the stage-setting for a violent act of defacement. But over and beyond these vaguely glimpsed but keenly felt motives, shaped and shared by the designers of automobiles, there was another order of ritual as set into the stage of divine justice. Yet one knew that no matter how many cars were trapped and rescued there would be more and that these four-wheel drive machines would busily transform nature, allowing people such as these, the eight-lighted ones, to get to places where previously only *campesinos* and *burros* had walked and waves licked the sand in rhythm to the moon. Was this why in this Elsewhere, not so much *industrialized* as *automobilized,* with the cities made unlivable on account of cars, there arose with the moon hanging high on the cliffs above the pounding sea the spirit queen, mistress of the serpents and dragons, ever more hemmed in by her ever more sacred wilderness on the horizon of human extremity in the crimson swathe left by the sun?

"The Death of the Monument" wrote the inimitable Lewis Mumford in his book, *The Culture of Cities* in 1938, convinced that the evanescent spirit of modernity was inimical to the monument. Perceiving an intimate connection between monumentalization and spirit possession, the monument being the outcome of the obsession of the living to perpetuate themselves after death, Mumford saw the monument as a throw-back to the worship of the House of the Dead, to civilizations and political thought-forms where death rang sure and true as weapon of obeisance. But now all that was going to disappear, and rightfully so. Invoking the sense of lightness and travel, mobility and nomadism, Mumford said our modern cities should be self-renewing organisms whose dominant image should not be the cemetery, where the dead must not be disturbed, but the field, meadow, and parkland

— things glowing with life, flat things, without a monument in sight, the dead whisked away.

But this drama of modernism pitting lightness and travel in opposition to the monument and The House of the Dead surely underestimates the curious affinity binding the opposition. Indeed, speed-and-control would seem to have a decisive need for monumentalization and the creation of sacred space.

Take the memorandum in the National Art Gallery dated December 1987 arguing for a restoration of the statue of the spirit queen that stands in the very center of the freeway running through the capital. Here, the House of the Dead and the modern city would seem to enhance one another no less than face off in mean-spirited opposition. Taking their life in their hands, devotees have for decades scurried across the path of several lanes of traffic to deposit their offerings and prayers to the thunderous applause of exhausts and shimmering car bodies.

Built by Alejandro Colina during the rule of the dictator in the early 1950s, the statue is remarkable for being so completely and utterly distinct from all other iconography of the spirit queen, normally depicted as a demure, European, Virgin Mary figure — but here as completely naked with huge tits and massive thighs clenched around the back of a large rodent-like creature with a notably oversized phallic-shaped snout, a Danta, denizen of the Amazon rain forest. At the same time as Colina was at work on this sculpture, be it noted, many of the state's favored icons and mythical figures were being rendered in a breathtaking high-camp elan, super-kitsch to beat the band, by Pedro Centeno Vallenilla encouraged, so it is said, by the dictator himself, to return to his native land to paint murals for the Capitol and the military headquarters in the capital city following his success in fascist Italy and Washington D.C. Building on folklore, but with a lusty eye for the naked body of the Indian and African, Centeno designed the ferocious Indian heads on the gold *cacique* coins minted since that time. It is these same heads that now stand forth as statues and portraits in the shops of magic across the nation. Centeno Vallenilla and artists like him adroitly exploited a colorful popular tradition for the sake of ruling passions. At the same time, the popular reappropiated this enriched authority.

Inspired by a deep passion for things Indian, Colina had as early as 1933 sculpted several grotesque Indians in a mystical setting at the country's main military base on the edge of the now polluted and sterile Lake Valencia, commissioned by the then president in the last years of his rule, the notorious Gómez, whose words of commemoration appear on a plaque expressing his profound admiration for the "aboriginal race." Despite Colina's good intentions, it is surely significant that it was during the two dictatorships of the twentieth century that he received commissions for substantial works of "Indian" statuary.

The memorandum in the National Art Gallery concerning the need to restore Colina's statue of the spirit queen in the middle of the city's freeway reads as follows:

> Its rarity, originality, and irreplaceable character give this monument a value justifying various measures aimed at rescuing and revalorizing it so that its importance can be diffused throughout the nation's culture. The material factors moulded by the spiritual force of the sculptor to create this testimony to our ancestry, this symbol now threatened by the city, where it was erected in a victorious gesture, these material factors are now minute by minute, succumbing to the very same forces which confront mankind.
>
> Sulfur dioxide, nitrogen dioxide, particulate matter such as carbon, soot, coal dust, lead, and carbon monoxide, are threatening the stability of the work and producing disassociation of its constituent materials, severely accentuated by the ceaseless vibration suffered by the pedestal bearing the weight which sustains the myth, now trembling and likely to lose part of its wholeness in an irreparable manner by the incessant and continuous passage at high speeds of the capital's traffic.

It's as if the statue itself were becoming possessed by traffic and modernity, shaking and trembling with the weight of the myth, even as it dies.

Colina himself was struck down by a car in the streets of the capital in 1972, incapacitated thereafter till his death. He died without realizing his project to make a nude copy of the Liberator offering the sword of justice to God.

He was a Darwinist and agnostic, his daughter said, with no belief whatsoever in the spirit queen. His first sculpture he did at the age of nineteen. It was called "The Indian's Grief."

It took almost an hour to travel the three miles to his daughter's apartment because of the traffic. It was impossible to get into her apartment building because it had been locked for security reasons, the intercom was broken, and there was no doorman. Luckily, cars came and went through the garage at the back, so one used that instead of the main entrance. There was no point in building doors for people any more. Maybe this mode of access prefigured the society as a whole, as a gigantic garage? Once inside Mission walked up several flights of stairs because the elevator was not working. Had it ever worked? Unfortunately once he arrived it was difficult to hear what she said. The floors were tiled and even though the windows were tightly shut, the noise from the traffic outside was deafening. Mission wondered how she made a living teaching opera singing and how she kept her good spirits given her view of the country as corrupt beyond words.

Freeways and the Sacred: the police barrier is not the only shrine to be found on the highway. There is also the cross by the side of the road marking death due to an accident.

These crosses are ubiquitous in Latin America, where cars constitute a leading cause of death. In Colombia, for instance, notorious for decades for all sorts of cruelty and violence, the third most common cause of death turns out to be not the AK 47 or the machete, but the murderous motor vehicle, and the vast majority of such deaths occur in cities. Car accidents not only cause more deaths than do heart attack or cancer; they also cause more deaths than the 5,000 killed per year in guerrilla warfare, drug-connected violence, and paramilitary assassination.

But while the latter are seen as acts of political violence, traffic accidents are not. In a curious way, these deaths are "accepted." This is a profoundly significant comment on modernity.

Indeed when a Colombian government official, Zaida Barrero de Noguera, on being interviewed recently about deaths due to automobiles said that "the roads in Colombia have been converted into scenes of war," she was able to make her point powerful because of the unexpectedness of the connection between driving a car and warfare. Seen not quite as "natural," like deaths due to heart attack or cancer, and yet not as socio-political either, such deaths and the disabilities associated with car accidents occupy a special preserve somewhere between nature and culture, a no-man's land where mechanical causes and the wrong side of fate rub shoulders in a bloody moment. The car accident — third or first world variety — is the modern equivalent of the miraculous gone awry, the moment where "it could have been all so different if only . . ." the moment where causation hangs in the balance and is found wanting, where chance transmutes into fate.

Some say these crosses are placed at the site of the accident for the purpose of remembrance. But then crosses are not placed where a person died of illness or of old age. Some say the cross is to pacify the aggrieved spirit which would otherwise bother the living — and the

same concern applies to the spirit of persons hanged, and to suicides. But why the placement of the cross at the site of the accident? Why can't the cross be placed over the corpse in the cemetery and be done with it?

No! It has to be at the actual physical site where the traffic accident — the *choque* — occurred, as well as at the cemetery. (The Spanish is useful here, using the same word *choque* for car collision as for shock, hence combining the two.)

In his famous essay on the representation of death written at the beginning of the century, the French ethnologist Robert Hertz concluded by observing that there were certain deaths that no amount of ritual could appease, and violent death was among them.

What we see here with the cross at the site of the *choque* is an excess above the norm of ritual effort, yet still no guarantee of stemming the flow of the "bloody moment."

In other words the roadside cross is compelled into existence as afterimage leaking sacred power, power that can in turn be augmented by more ritual effort.

It was a hot August afternoon with the sun low in the sky by the highway winding between the two towns nearest the magic mountain. There were two trucks pulled up. The young drivers were in that compacted semi-trance posture drawing in deep draughts on their *tabacos* by a beautiful shrine made of three peak-roofed doll's house chapels side by side, about eight foot high.

"How did this shrine come into being?" Mission asked.

A truck driver had died in flames in a *choque* on this very curve, they said. A cross had been erected. Some other truck driver came along, asked the spirit to grant him a favor, and the spirit carried out the request. The spirit listened! The spirit paid heed.

From that point on a cult developed and people built a more and more elaborate shrine; in his little house, candles flaming, the Indio Guaicaipuro; the spirit queen in her sanctuary, to the right; and the venerable doctor José Gregorio Hernández in the center.

Carrying the goods back and forth across this sunny land—oil out; cars, ammo, and videos in—truck drivers are the primordial force knitting the circulation of commodities together in a magical network of death—shrines encrusted in death's afterglow emanating from the sacrifices in *choques* they make with their own bodies to the national economy. Take these *carnets* (the term also used for an identification card as issued by the state) of a truck driver, Domingo Antonio Sánchez, purchased in a shop of magic. His face changes with different cards. In one he looks like a police identikit. He was a singular man and yet his magical soul as conveyed by the pictures of his face when alive is strangely multiple and scored with the spiritual force of anonymity, as has been the fate of the Virgin or Jesus, let alone of the dead Indians and Blacks and the Liberator himself as they pass into Canetti's crowd of the dead. On the back of the image of the face there is this prayer.

PRAYER TO BROTHER DOMINGO ANTONIO SANCHEZ

Oh! Spirit DOMINGO ANTONIO SANCHEZ! *You who voyaged back and forth on the country's highways you knew like the back of your hand, driving your truck to support your family!*

You, the exemplary driver, as generous with your fellow truckies as with car drivers!

One day you lost your life on the highway Carora Puente Torres. Your companions, who race the highways, built you a chapel so they can meet with you and light a candle.

As you were dying, this is what you said. "I will care for any driver who has faith in me, especially for those who get into an accident."

The person who reads this prayer or carries it on their person will be always protected by me.

Go with God, driver. One Our Father and Ave Maria.

The magical impact of shock comes from something more than its being a cause, as *choque*, of violent death that spills over into the

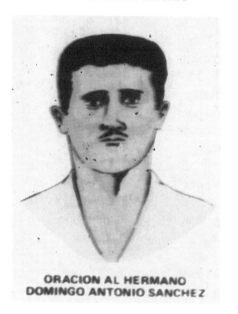

**ORACION AL HERMANO
DOMINGO ANTONIO SANCHEZ**

beyond where no rest obtains. With its somersaulting movement of remembrance and amnesia, its swarming stasis of anticipation and reflection, shock also sums up as process and effect what is at stake in magic's journey through time. Indeed, as regards the human body, shock's magic is no less an exploration of time than it is a type of historiography, and a crucially important one, at that. Marcel Mauss caught some of this where he implied that magic is not only a reaction to shock but a component of it as well, that when the habitual is disturbed, shock may be triggered and — as he put it — "society hesitates, searches, waits."

The hesitation, its tension and hope, its ruffling of the imagination through the concatenation of chance and tragedy occasioned by violent physical impact is very much the sign of modernity too, as Wolfgang Schivelbusch reminds us when he elaborates on the new human physiology of shock-rhythm in the European nineteenth-century railway journey as both fact and metaphor of the modern. In his "Theses on the Philosophy of History," written in Paris on the eve of the second world war and shortly before his despair at the thought of being captured by the Gestapo drove him to suicide in Port Bou, Walter Benjamin traced what he saw as a particularly crucial contour of physical shock in the realm of modern thought and philosophy of history, thus: "Thinking involves not only the flow of thoughts, but their arrest as well. Where thinking suddenly stops in a configuration pregnant with tensions, it gives that configuration a shock, by which it crystallizes into a monad."

The interpreter as "historical materialist," he went on, approaches a historical subject, only where it is encountered as a monad.

And what is a monad?

A monad is an absolute oneness where divinity and the impossibility of such oneness combine. It is the moment of death-stillness so quiescent and calm that it no less prefigures than belies the terrible energy within, a unity where there can be none, explosive with the promise of redemption.

And how does one find such a monad or recognize it when it presents itself?

Is it not the case that the monad takes the form of an image of the fixed-explosive made famous by surrealism with its abutment of dissimilars in a forcefield of shock — of which the cross by the highway no less than the locomotive brought to rest in the forest is the crudest, albeit quintessential, instance? And is it not further the case that the whole point of such monadism is its relation to time-forms, its coagulating and liquefying of time-crystals in relation to real history, bearing in mind Hegel's triangulated observation that history is as much the form of its telling as it is actual events and that in this peculiar duplicity history only comes into being with the coming into being of the state itself in which, finally, reason has displaced God as the mechanism articulating the particular to the general?

But the point is that the articulation can never be achieved, no matter how much the spirits of the dead are ransacked for their treasure. Monadism haunts quite other laws of history where meaning lies in wait as embodied, nervous impulse, prior to the leap into the unknown where "not even the dead shall be safe." Modernity has created a graveyard of failed attempts with half-polished shards of reason adrift on junk piles of discarded ceremonial outbursts.

In contemplating this self-absorbing power wrought from assemblages of violence and death, it is daunting the degree to which the mystique of the originary violence of the conquest and of the anti-colonial wars has in popular iconography blended with the violence of the modern. For together with the state-endorsed heroes such as the Liberator on his white horse, and together with the enigmatic spirit queen hanging high like the rising moon above the crimson sea, mistress of the serpents and the dragons, who can forget the specter of the saint most esteemed throughout this land, the venerable doctor José Gregorio Hernández, struck dead by a car as he crossed the street in the capital in 1919.

15

—— *Faith in Marble*

Lustrous and smooth.
Impenetrable.
Heavy enough to make the ships creak and toss.
And very expensive.

We are talking Marble—stately being in its forthright mood, mottled with a tortured history, bulging veins expending themselves in meandering frenzies such that, on a quiet day, ear pressed to the cold surface, you might still hear the earth's growling, its unseemly hand-wringing compression. But now behold it in its serenity; excavated and chiseled, cool to the eyeball no less than to the fingertips, freed from the hot earth. Like bronze, good for statues.

"In the plazas there are busts and statues representing him," reads a commentary from 1942. "On days of unrest, on days of alarm, on days of great resolutions, on days of jubilation, the crowd gathers around his effigy, image of the father surrounded by the love and confidence of his offspring. The contemplation of his statue seems to elevate and dignify the thought of men."

The sculptor sees the form hidden in the marble. The sculptor creates the mould from the idea into which the molten bronze is poured. The effort is there straining to burst through, as if the substantial substance highlights by antithesis the sublime transcendence of the idea the substance restrains and figures. A statue is a site for philosophical meditation, where force and image lock together.

Spirit possession shares these properties of the statue.

Spirit possession embodies idea and the ideals too, encasing them in the gesticulating human frame, in the *caja*, or box, of the body, as it is called. Even more graphic is the use of the word *materia* to mean the human body as substance, as that which is ready after much purification to receive and hence materialize spirits.

The resemblance to the statue is readily apparent in the *velación* where the human body lies spreadeagled in its halo of flame in front of a shrine, so quiet, so unbearably still, this inert body gathering itself as purity defined as pure matter so as to be one day inhabited by a spirit, except here, unlike the statue, the body lies horizontal, stretched out along the earth's surface. Only when animated and brought to life by the spirit does the figure become erect. But in its prolonged immobility stretched along the ground the body passes, as it were, into a death-trance. It becomes corpse-like which is something more and less than death, the corpse being but the beginning, the materialization of death which, with the funeral rites and the passing away of the flesh then becomes empty but empowered, filled with active non-materiality—with memory, image, and spirit.

The corpse is a powerful site of abjection and taboo, a sacred power, morbid and ambivalent tilted, like the spirit queen herself, towards evil, harbinger of a reflux, maybe, the reflux of beneficient power, but certainly charged like a spring compressed in the utter stillness of this corpse-performance collapsing giant rhythms of quietude and decay into staged proportion of telescoped time under the weeping trees — the stillness marking the time of the nothing in which nothing changes or shall change; this is one time.

The other time intersecting with this is the time of beautification of the corpse laid down upon the filigree of baby-powder in front of the vivid colors and figures on the shrine. Around this burns the halo, divine rays of light proceeding from the candles implanted upright in the earth around the body.

All this the corpse of the live body concentrates into itself. Religion depends upon posture.

Such materialization-and-spiritualization at one and the same time parallels the move from marble to figure we witness in the statue. Because of this transcendence, people do not say spirit *possession* but *transportation*, and with this abundant sense of flight we discern another factor in the embodiment of stately being, not the hard impenetrability of marble but the mobile fluidity of the mass, the people, the *pueblo* within the armor of stately marble. Spirit possession thus draws as much upon the transformative and fanciful aspects in state representation as it does on the hardness of marble and bronze,

using the dead in combination with the living human body in order to stage ductility no less than literalization.

In the early years of the Soviet Union, as a powerful gesture toward a people's state iconography, Lenin favored impermanent statuary made from fragile or soft materials such as plaster of paris instead of marble, bronze, or granite. In the European Elsewhere, possessed of the spirit queen's enchanted mountain, we can already discern such evanescence in the countless shops of magic in every city and town down to the smallest villages where plaster of paris rules the day in a riot of figurational impulse — precisely the same tumult of forms occurring with spirit possession on the mountain.

All this evanescence fading in, fading out, flare and ephemerality, is in keeping with the being-and-nothingness of the Spirit Queen — counterposed, to be sure, by His steadfastness. Even when cast in plaster of paris, He is painted to look like bronze. In contrast to this studied machining of the stately-real, she is moody presence, the swirling medium that defies representation. Sure, there are pictures and statues of her. But with the exception of one haunting image of her as the center of the Three Potencies, they always seem to be statements that she cannot be represented — and even this startling image of the Three Potencies, on account of its hauntedness, should be thought of this way. That is why she is best represented not by a work of art but by the mountain, and it is not so much the mountain as silhouetted form but as mass, as bulk, as irregularity in the mass, that is here important.

She provides both ineffability and representational space, by which I mean she exists not so much as a figure but as the possibility for figuration. Meanwhile, His task is to pin-point, to fix, to center, to cut a sharp silhouette in space — and it is destiny that He be there in marble and bronze or fake marble and fake bronze in every hamlet, village, town, and city across the territory. She is the substance-less medium prefiguring and necessary to all representation, while the Liberator is the form of forms. Together they interlock to create the theater of spirit-literalization — yet the people, unlike Lenin, want the permanence and clarity that comes with marble.

"I want him in marble even though it will cost me more," she said. "In marble you see him more clearly. I have faith in marble."

So does the state.

Perhaps because the harder the substance, the more evanescent the spirit it houses. Take the state monument at Carabobo, virtual center-piece of the state's staging spirit possession, built to commemorate what is claimed to be the decisive victory of the anti-colonial war. Even for a Nation-State packed solid with statues of the Liberator and other notable men and horses of liberation this monumental complex is impressive. Less than fifty miles from the enchanted mountain of the spirit queen, it was built in 1921 by the most famous of all dictators, Juan Vicente Gómez, who after he died in 1935, came to be known as *The Tyrant*. In 1930 he built an addition to Carabobo to commemorate the centenary of the death of the Liberator. It stands therefore as a fine example, a monumental example, we might say, of how the magic of the state is saturated by death, doubly so in that Gómez himself comes down through history, as told, as the greatest killer of all time, famous for his bone-chilling tyranny (which has served as a foil for later democratic regimes to obscure their own) and, like all presidents, is said to have illicitly maintained contact with the spirit queen.

The stories are legion, postscripts to mythologies involving still older stories, the killer-man and the spirit queen at the center of the secrets of state, yet nevertheless it is still a shock to occasionally come across his perky little statue on shrines at her mountain. Nothing, it would seem, could more effectively clear the field of illusions as to the Christian piety embedded in these manifestations of popular culture, no matter how much she looks like the Virgin Mary. With Gómez as a saint, if not a god, there is little room for cheap sen-

Juan Vicente

INVOCACION

Ofrezco estas santas luces, con el permiso del gran poder de Dios,
la Santísima Trinidad, Corte Celestial y Santos del Cielo, en especial a
este hermano.
A la Corte Libertadora en esta hora y en este momento, para que
con su fuerza y este poder me den luz y protección; venciendo así todo obstáculo de cualquier índole que se presenta para tener fuerza y
valor y salir adelante en cualquier momento y circunstancia que se
presente el problema, sea monetario, de protección, de salud y de cru-
zamiento, para que con tu sable poderoso y protector poder, así salir
hacia adelante en todo.
Récese un Padre Nuestro a nombre de este hermano, tres Ave María, a nombre de su espíritu protector y guía.

timentality and childish hopes as to redemption following suffering, or
of virtue and humility finding reward.

Carabobo: High on horseback the Liberator stands on a mountain of
dead surveying the arch of triumph erected over the tomb to the
unknown soldier. Death-statuary in granite and marble weighs heavily
on the extended plain covered with white concrete. "The larger and
more frequent the heaps of dead which a survivor confronts, the
stronger and more insistent becomes his need for them," says
Canetti in *Crowds and Power*.

Concrete and Modernism: Marble is dead! Long live Marble! Long
live death. But power-centralized is also power-diffused and horizontal
like the bodies gathering force in the *velación* in front of the shrines
on her enchanted mountain. Now comes concrete—the marble of
democracy and republican government, the "poor man's marble of
modernity," spreading its skirts over the blood-soaked battlefield
where *El Negro* Felipe, faithful to the end, fought barefoot. Unlike marble, concrete can be poured over everything and anywhere, symmetri-
calizing an ever more fluid world. Forget the "carpenter frame of reference" as that startling contrast with grass huts and loopy circular
structures of real primitives at home with the birds and the rising of
the evening star. Instead think modern with the "concrete frame of reference" flowing from marble outcrops of the dead planted on the car-

nage of the originary violence. Forget the ground. Forget the underground. It's all a matter of cement gushing across the face of the earth in elaborate traceries bracing the territory in hardening grids and tunnels of user-friendly monumentation. Think concretely! Marble is dead! *¡Que viva el marmol!*

Magic Mountain: Like the magic mountain, the monumental state complex at Carabobo derives its power from harnessing the unquiet souls of the dead. Despite the differences, the enchanted mountain is based on this stately model no less than the mountain is the model on which Carabobo is itself based.

The sheer immensity declares that here in Carabobo nature is dominated by the strict vision of the "state apparatus." The endless sterile surface of concreted nature over which one walks to the Arch of Triumph towering over the Tomb to the Unknown Soldier allows of no disorder, no meandering along twisting pathways skirting unruly shrubs, convoluted roots, and boulders strewn higgeldy-piggeldy by insistent streams and eye-riveting *portales* or shrines. Here at Carabobo there is no sodden refuse nor butterflies unpredictably zigzagging in schools of dazzling color attracted by human shit and the supernatural force of the dead. The whole point, one could say, of the stately design is obsessional, as opposed to excremental, holding tight as opposed to spending, maintenance of taboo as opposed to its transgression, negation as opposed to the negation of the negation.

But even this is an over-simplification, for surely the power of the state monument as that which maintains taboo lies also in transgressing taboo, engaging in corpse-performance so as to animate stately being. With the official there is undulating movement of partial exposures back and forth across the taboo, a sort of strip-tease of history as violent memory, quiescent but brooding under heavy formalities of stately granite and concrete — violating the taboos relevant to killing and to corpse-performance that make humans human, while simultaneously observing those very same taboos and thus creating a spill-over of stately awe.

The body is a critical index here. At Carabobo the point is to maintain the spectator's body erect like a statue parallel to the might of granite-in-death in a performance of rigidity — while on the mountain the body is no longer that of a spectator but is instead the body of the spectacle, the corpse-vehicle of transportation bared to the serenity no less than to the wildness of spirit expending itself to cacophonies of drumbeats and "*Fuerza! Fuerza!*" as the body, once possessed by spirit, cavorts and side-slips into cut-out silhouettes through the flames and forests of symbols guarding the gates of the shrine snuggled into the rock's crevice or the tree's gnarled roots. The rhythm here is of the montaged unit of speed cutting out rapidly changing spaces against the sky's blackness — an arhythmic crossing of the moving sea of existence, drunkenly gesticulating like a marionette twisting between the smooth hardness of its marble-form and the

organic flexibility of its human body-form let loose, a statue come to life but not sure of how or why, legs twisting at the knees, elbows forced inwards, eyes staring. Yes! This is a quite different bodily relation to the sacred than that demanded by stately presence as at Carabobo (a word which *literally* means face of the fool) where the two bodies face off, the looker and the looked at, the human statue and the stone statue, erect, firm, unyielding, cleaving the space of the sky in an unbearable quiet broken only by breathing and the whisper of the occasional passing cloud.

And surely the Arch of Triumph is a *portal*, too? Arnold Van Gennep tells us as much in his famous little book on rites of passage published at the beginning of the twentieth century. The word *arch* is synonymous with *portal,* and the *portal* is the veritable origin in Western culture of the form used to signify the passage from one state of being to another. The Arch of Triumph erected by the state is simply the magnification of this, he says. But we may want to explore this further for we see in this development not only a continuity of the fusion of warrior and priest in the composite form of the king, the emperor, and modern state itself, but also an ever-tighter identification of the magic of the state with warring being and a solicitation of death such that the Arch of Triumph comes to stand for the passage of statehood-becoming.

But there we must go, penetrating the impenetrable marble at last. A short sprint across the Tomb of the Unknown Soldier. Legs pumping. Defilement. Through the Arch of Triumph, that great cunt of brawny legs, the man become a statue. The Unknown Soldier has escaped in yet another brilliant performance of hidden innerness.

Guarded as it is by unmoving troops in scarlet uniforms and ceremonial swords, it is nevertheless the very nature of the sacred to leak. "Behind all these prohibitions," wrote our man in Vienna in 1912 (sucking heavily on a *tabaco*), "behind all these prohibitions there seems to be something in the nature of a theory that they are necessary because certain persons and things are charged with a dangerous power, which can be transferred through contact with them, almost like an infection." He was at pains to point out in this regard the closeness if not identity of *taboo, sacred, unclean, dangerous,* and *uncanny,* and went on to note that some people or things have more of this dangerous power than others and that the danger is proportional to the difference of potential of the charges. Hence the centrifugal flow or, should we say, "leak" of spirits from the state's inner core of monotheistic being to the lesser charged regions surrounding and abounding — hence this leak from the emptiness of the spiritual tumult of the Tomb of the Unknown Soldier sustaining the Arch of Triumph pressing down on the earth, reaching for the sky.

For here in this entombed writhing of spirited emptiness we confront the phantom point of coalescence and separation where, to make the state of the whole truly whole, the profane must meet, but cannot meet, the sacred in crackling discharge of holy fire — where, to quote a founding father of sociology writing in the same year as our Viennese magus but in the city of Paris from and to where so much stately modeling has been imported and exported by European Elsewheres, to quote on this vexing matter of the contagiousness of the sacred, "the profane environment and the sacred one are not merely distinct, but they are also closed to one another; between them there is an abyss. So there ought to be some particular reason in the nature of sacred things, which causes this exceptional isolation and mutual exclusion."

"And in fact," he continues, "*by a sort of contradiction* (the emphasis is mine) the sacred world is inclined, *as it were* (again my emphasis), to spread itself into this same profane world which it excludes elsewhere: at the same time that it repels it, it tends to flow into it as soon as it approaches. This is why it is necessary to keep them at a distance from one another and to create a sort of vacuum between them."

As it were. Inclined to spread itself at the same time as it repels. . . . What sort of *contradiction* is this? The "contradiction" of "the sacred" better stated as not only dealing with gods, rites, and prohibitions, but first and foremost with the restless energy of a mysterious force overflowing with the ceaseless power of attraction and repulsion? "Contradiction" barely begins to get at this and that is why we put this force first, this force that both structures and dissolves itself before our eyes when we think of "the sacred." And nowhere is this more frenetic as a mysterious force for structuring and destructuring than when it comes to power and violence in the form of stately authority far away or right at home. Imagine the tension within this movement spreading at the same time as it repels here at the source in the shadow under the Arch where lies the Tomb. Is it possible to maintain this abyss of tension between dissemination and repulsion other than by a continuous torment of movement, a constant evacuation of its nothingness in a never-ending pursuit of a body?

Imagine this Tomb of the Unknown Soldier, the privileged space of death founding the state of the whole, spilling forth spirit after spirit from its cavernous interior and, instead of *shrinking* with each expenditure, *expanding* with each escape to freedom, evacuating like crazy in order to create the impossible but necessary space between — and the more the sacred expends itself, seeping like the concrete from the marble across the sovereign territory, the more spirits have to be evacuated to make the vacuum vacuuminous. The Tomb to the Unknown soldier would thus be bottomless and the world of spirit no less than of flesh preeminently a world on the march, unstable, unstoppable.

Imagine these spirits passing forth from the tomb like winged angels across sovereign territory, drawn to the enchanted mountain rearing from the plain, to pass forth there as images into flesh, quivering, unsure of what's expected.

Nietzsche reminds us of the passing away of metaphor into a type of literality, into the illusion of truth itself, canonical and binding. Thus the greatest art in the everyday art of truth-making is the art of self-concealment of that art, the dying away of metaphor and figure to remain, at best, a ghost-like presence haunting the realness of reality.

But now the ghost emerges from the tomb full-bodied and winged in search of other theaters — theaters of bodies and embodiment where metaphor, reinvigorated, seeks literalization in order to remain alive with the haunting power of death.

"They've jumped the abyss, goddammit!"

Just a quick hop and a jump from the marble tomb to her mountain-mass.

Flecked with the flight of spirits lifting off from the flight-deck of the battlefield searching for her mountain, a troubled sky reflects the pools and rivulets turbulent with their passage across the length and breadth of the state of the whole. The leak spreads despite repulsion along waterways, drains, and filmy sky-trails into an unquenchable flow searching for body, first hers, then yours. This adds resonance to atmosphere dense with aftermaths of spirit movement through bodies. The humid air hangs heavy with promise. Indeed it is to *movement* defined as contagion, not to source or essence, that, according to the aforementioned theory of religion we find sacred being which, in effect, becomes a massive movement of circulation, a contagion, rippling in unpredictable stops and starts through a vast heterogeneity of substances, stages, and sites that, by virtue of the efferevescently transformative rippling-through tunnels, prison walls, school text-book pictures, newspaper editorials, postage stamps, names of insurance companies, universities, bus companies, statues, plazas, school murals, police stations, mustaches, money, memory, and the corpse, gives definitive spiritual form to the state of the whole.

The passageway to the Arch of Triumph is lined by sixteen black statues, eight a side, each on its white pedestal, one for every famous military leader of the anti-colonial wars of the early nineteenth century.

There is, however, one of the sixteen statues in front of the arch of triumph that is not a military officer.

Just the name appears.

Pedro Camejo.

And then underneath that is engraved, *Negro Primero*, the same figure who appears as thus named or as *El Negro* Felipe in so many shrines on the enchanted mountain some fifty miles from his official presentation by the state on this battlefield and whom Katy so loved.

But while the soldiers in the brilliant red uniforms of the founding violence tirelessly occupy themselves in the exaction of prohibition and revelation in the stately strip-tease of the corpse, there on the magic mountain the semi-naked pilgrims are able to rework that theater of taboo and transgression and redouble the magic of the state by offering the hospitality of their shrines no less than of their bodies

☐ — *Pedro Primero*
at Carabobo

☐ — *Pedro Primero*
folk statue

□ — *As one of*
Las Tres Potencias

to the refugees fleeing the Tomb in staggered impulses of dissemination and repulsion. There, also dressed for the main part in red, now seen as the color of Indians (whom the tyrant Juan Vicente admired so much), of warring and of valor, the pilgrims to the enchanted mountain flesh out the spirit of good and evil underlying stately being. Thus with their gesticulating, inwards twisting, bodies, they deal with the enemy, exorcise sorcery, poverty, envy, and sickness, by becoming Other in the great drama, tragic and absurd, of the Nation-State, its timeless truth, operatic and melodramatic, no less saintly than wicked.

PART THREE —— # THE THEATER OF DIVINE JUSTICE

SIMON BOLIVAR
LIBERTADOR I PADRE DE LA PATRIA

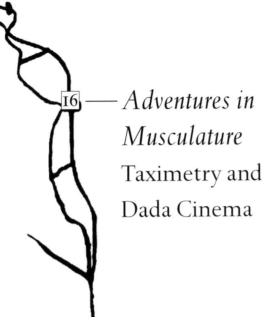

16

— *Adventures in Musculature* Taximetry and Dada Cinema

Just a small encounter heading west the day before Christmas 1987 in the Ford *Conquistador*, the biggest car Hertz had for hire. It was a modern-day *conquistador*, very wide, very white, nicely chromed and air-conditioned against the harsh elemental force of a vengeful nature. Suspended on soaring springs we floated like a cloud down the highway.

The wind whistled in from the grey ocean. Spume was driven off the waves into piles of foam quavering on the edge of dissolution on the deserted beach shimmering in the heat. Every now and again a car appeared like a mirage through the heat to hiss in smooth streaks of sound along the highway melting into the distance along the edge of the sand.

Between the beach and the highway, the country's ashphalted testimony to modernity, lay broken-down cinder-block huts used as restaurants and bars by beach-goers from nearby towns and the capital itself.

We stopped where a small, foxy, white man with a Firestone baseball cap was sitting and we ordered some beer and fish which the Black woman inside started to fry.

"Where are you from?" he asked, with the authority of ownership. We told him we'd been in the magic mountain (some two-hours drive away), and his face clouded.

"You shouldn't have taken your children there," he said. It was dangerous because spirits could steal them or make them sick.

He shook his head at our disbelief.

"Where do you come from?" he asked again.

We kidded around with our accented Spanish. "From Costaguana," we said, because indeed we spent a good part of our lives there and because it felt good to find a place that could, in the circumstances, only be confusing, now we were playing the nationalist game.

Given the look on his face struggling between disbelief and diplomacy, we added, "No, we're not" His face lightened.

"I don't like Costaguanians," he said.

Just a little guy enjoying his chauvinism by the sea with a bunch of foreigners waiting for a woman frying fish. In his mind's eye Mission could see him Firestone cap and all at the magic mountain spreadeagled on the nation's flag becoming possessed by the Liberator and surrounded by Indians in red shorts.

"Why not?"

"Because when the war comes the Costaguanians living here will form a fifth column."

It was weird. Not *if* there is a war with Costaguana, the stuff of stately discourse; newspaper headlines saber-rattling frothing at the mouth state having a fit — No! This was altogether calm and beyond that. The definitive, omniscient, *when* there is a war. . . .

It seemed like he knew something the rest of us didn't and this being in on the secret allowed him a measure of repose. Where did he get this "fifth column" stuff from? Shades of revolutionary melodrama, witch-hunts, the enemy within. Fifth column indeed!

It turned out that in the 1950s he'd been an intelligence operative serving in the President's newly created national security police, the SN, to all accounts a nasty bunch.

"What sort of things did you do as an intelligence operative?" Mission asked as the wind whistled in from the dull sea and every now and again a car streaked along the highway, inches from their rickety table.

His answer was breath-taking, so simple, so unexpected. For a moment the piles of foam the wind had whipped off the waves onto the beach stopped wobbling.

He worked as a taxi-driver in the capital, he said, listening to his passengers, taking note of their journeys, and urging them on in conversation so as to plumb their thoughts.

We ate the fish, got back into our *Conquistador,* and Charles gunned it down the highway to Coro.

It's so true it's cliché — and isn't the cliché that very thing which circulates, sums up, and gathers power from circulation? — that the first thing strangers do when they arrive in a new place is to ask the taxi driver for the inside story, what's really going on, the secrets that determine the shape of the national situation. It's as if the driver is credited with proximity to some not just hidden but mysterious core of information and feeling, ranging from affairs of the heart to secrets of state because the driver has been in so many places and carried so many different people.

For a short time both stranger and driver will share the same, enclosed, moving space, isolated yet part of the traffic circulating around them, winding their way through congestion past homes, parks, monuments, office buildings, shops, and warehouses. The stranger is a vessel to be filled and is paying for a service. The stranger is weak and ignorant in many ways, but the stranger has a certain aura too, and this is one reason why the taxi driver may talk — somewhat like an informant enjoying talking to an anthropologist.

The stranger's vulnerability may draw the driver closer. The stranger instinctively appreciates this and milks the driver for information and secret understandings of "the situation." "Is the president still popular?" "What are people thinking?" And so forth. These large-scale issues become all the more impressive for being intertwined with small-scale personal philosophies and speculations in the intimate strangeness that is the cab.

This is why the man with the Firestone cap, deftly turning the tables, was such a revelation. Inserted into *the popular* by *the official,* he uses popular custom and the dialectic subtlety of understandings on which it is based to circulate that understanding into military intelligence. He takes advantage of those who would take advantage not so much of him personally but of taxying through modernity with its brief flash of contact made intimate in the anonymity of the city.

The word taxi comes from taximeter, just as the word cab (as in taxi-cab) comes from the hansom cabs mounted with metering devices computing money in terms of distance traveled in Berlin, Paris, and London at the turn of the century. Precisely because this is a strictly financial and urban transaction, the driver and the stranger are bound by a personal and potentially mystical bond—a bond that is not the hang-over of tradition, but is manufactured by the modern itself. The man with the Firestone cap was a man whose time in history had come. His importance lies in his evoking for us strangers the nature and some of the depths traversed by the circulation between the popular and the stately.

And just as important, through the surprise of the revelation, through the sudden reversal, he reminds us that circulation, no less than revelation, is bound to intermittence, transposition, and shock.

Revelation implies de-masking as an Enlightenment inversion of medieval practice, and de-masking implies circulation but gives it a special twist; something new is added as the mask gathers its tensed power from the public secret it fabricates, while de-masking gathers this power, circulating the behind to the front. If this seems overly complex, take the case of the state and the way it lends itself to the language of masks in the turbulent slipstream of political theology— as in the work of the late Philip Abrams who tells us that the state is not the reality which stands behind the mask of political practice. *It is itself the mask* which prevents our seeing political practice as it is.

But what, then, without needlessly prolonging the epistemic anxiety this arouses, what is it we see, seeing as how we are prevented from seeing? Beginning from illusion, how would we ever be sure of disillusion? How is it that what appears to be the mask—ie., "political practice"—is really the behind, while what is presumably the behind— ie., "the state"—turns out to be the mask itself?

The taxi driver turns to stare us in the face.

The confusing figure of the mask is helpful only so long as, instead of trying to rip it off, we recognize and even empathize with its capacity to confuse, which means we take stock of the fact that what's important is not that it conceals but that it makes truth.

We might call this the "mask-effect" with its strange facility of seeming to make sense, for an instant, then losing its comprehensibility, only to regain it, and thus maintain a wave-like or circular motion in which the component elements—reality and unreality, front and behind, masking and demasking, our seeing and our not seeing— keep changing places. And while the magic mountain provides the theater of this theater, what exists in Nation-States without such an elaborated stage is nevertheless the same vertiginous waves of impulses thus extended from the official to the unofficial spheres of society, and back again.

Franz Kafka saw the adventures of musculature no less than the twisting movement of air and music in the submission to command that this involved. It was 1911. The place: the Yiddish Theater Troupe in Prague. "It made my cheeks tremble," he wrote with reference to the representative of the government, one of the few Christians in the hall, "a wretched person afflicted with a facial tic that — especially on the left side of his face, but spreading also far onto the right — contracts and passes from his face with almost merciful quickness, I mean the haste, but also the regularity, of the second hand. When it reaches the left eye it almost obliterates it. For this contraction new, small, fresh muscles have developed in the otherwise quite wasted face. The talmudic melody of minute questions, adjurations or explanations: the air moves into a pipe and takes the pipe along, and a great screw, proud in its entirety, humble in its turns, twists from small, distant beginnings in the direction of the one who is questioned."

The tic moves with the haste but also the regularity of the second hand across the facial wasteland in a twisting melody confounding the great binaries of matter and spirit by transmuting substance with image so as to form assemblages — such as those to be found as shrines or "gateways" on the spirit queen's mountain. The most pronounced of these assemblages of course is the full blown ritual of possession itself in which rite establishes the equivalence between image and spirit, the rite fixing spirit into the human body through variegated image-impulsions in a series of shock-like contractions beginning in the legs and arms and moving to the center of the body and the head, especially the eyes and tongue.

There exist models a-plenty for thinking about this perplexing translation between sign and force, matter and spirit, and perhaps all religions can be thought of as attempts at harnessing the energy locked therein. Dada cinema presents a newer model, appropriate to the modernity of the magic mountain.

Thomas Elsaesser provides us with a way of thinking about Dada cinema which fits both with the spirit queen's magic mountain and with the place of that mountain in the circulation of energy and signs in stately being. He tells us that cinema occasioned amongst Dadaists a model not only for representing the body in relation to the social environment, but also for getting across the notion of the artwork as an event, not as an object "but as circuits of exchange for different energies and intensities, for the different aggregate states matter can be subjected to between substance and sign through an act of transposition, assemblage, division, and intermittence."

This engaging attitude towards the staggering back and forth transfer between impulse and image suggests the outlandish but real possibility that underpinning the legitimacy of the modern state is a vast movement of transposition between the official and the unofficial for which spirit possession is paradigmatic.

This circulation between the official and the unofficial implicates language itself. Indeed, figuration presupposes circulation.

When, for instance, the President of the republic invokes (as he has to) the spirit of the Liberator on public occasions — as will every schoolteacher and minor official across the land — we might, on reflection, want to understand this as a figurative, rhetorical, poetic, turn of speech. He doesn't really mean it, we might say. It's a (mere) "turn" of phrase, a poetic "flight" and therefore in some terribly real sense unreal. Yet to say that is to "fly in the face" (speaking of metaphor) of the make-believe required for the power of figuration — the make-believe that insists that indeed in some crazy yet totally necessary way the figure (of speech) could in some significant sense be real and concrete or partake at some crucial moment in its poetic making for the blessed touch of the real, as for instance with incongruous blendings and assemblages, in themselves unlikely, but constituted by real possibilities and reaching out to larger, novel, truths, as happens so remarkably in the case of the spiritual underpinning of the Nation-State on the magic mountain where the spirits of the dead are literalized and where to be possessed by history is a fact of matter no less than matter of fact.

Metaphor is, in other words, essential to the artwork by which the sense of the literal is created and its power captured. As to the nature of this artwork, the great wheel of meaning is here not only state-based but based on an artistic death in which metaphor auto-destructs giving birth to literality whose realness achieves its emphatic force through being thus haunted. The real is the corpse of figuration for which body-ritual as in spirit-possession is the perfect statement, providing that curious sense of the concrete that figure and metaphor need — while simultaneously perturbing that sense with one of performance and make-believe in the "theater of literalization."

Moving across the wasteland of the face that is at once both the window to the soul and its mask, the tic of official rhetoric is empowered by the ghost haunting the real which, as the magic of the state, is extracted by unofficial rites of spirit possession in which ghosts are allowed, albeit in enclosed space, to openly rejoin the living. We are talking here of nothing less than the social basis of figuration and hence of the carnal quality to language itself, and it needs to be noted that the necessary distinctions between the dead and the living, no less than between the official and unofficial are, to some crucial extent, class and race ordained distinctions as it is, by and large, the poor, especially the urban poor, who fulfill this desperate need for a body. It is these poor whose task it is to supply stately discourse with its concrete referents; pre-historic dream images of Indians and Blacks entangled in the first-world romance of the colony, that Elsewhere animated by first-world exotica circulating as spirit power haunting the bodies of the living, first time tragedy . . .

Cacique Naiguatá

Such bodily takeover by the dead bespeaks an infinity of life through the medium of the beautified corpse which no state these days of sad decline in the body politic can risk to ignore. Even the Chief Justice — especially the Chief Justice — acknowledges this, even as he frets about the desecration of the flag and taking things a little too literally. His thoughts gravitate to the spirit queen. The problem lies right there, he decides, with the impulse to desecration so ready at hand in matters of state as absolute spirit strives frantically with the mute absurd to balance the competing claims of violence and reason. This is a subtle point, he figures, that the magic is in the state itself and not in the magical thinking of the citizenry. Still there's no denying that from there it's just a short step to where people get into the act willingly and are able to make magic from it, allowing their very bodies to blur with the spiritual power of the state in horrendous displays of mimetic excess. To become possessed by the spirit of a sixteenth century *cacique!* By an early nineteenth century barefoot black cowboy freedom fighter! By the Liberator himself, coughing blood! And then there's the mood! The mood is everything. To become possessed by that. To generate that. And did you see the size of that flag! And the needles through the cheeks with the national colors? Those bottomless eyes and vacant stares? . . .

The Chief has deliberated a great deal about the symbols of state and where they fit into freedom of speech doctrine. He has cast his thought wide and deep about the separation of Church from State, yet still feels dissatisfied about the status of these symbols. Are they sacrosanct? Surely. But how could they be sacred with the state so emphatically secular? Could it be that the symbols of the emphatically non-sacred are themselves profoundly sacred? A page of history is worth a volume of logic (Justice Holmes). His head whirls. There is a historically created vacuum here. A space too empty for its own good. *Desecration!* Yes! When they desecrate symbols of state, then the sacred emerges and emerges no longer as symbol but with bodily force. But how strange, muses the Chief Justice, how strange that here only the negative exists and we never openly declare the symbols of state sacred. It's like a secret, cheating the gods of their rightful domain, or maybe conspiring with them.

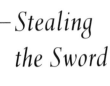

17 — *Stealing the Sword*

The stealing of the Liberator's sword in January 1974 was the first public action by the M-19 *guerrilla*, their baptism, so to speak and their leap onto the stage of history.

Alvaro Fayad, general commander of the M-19, later tortured, released, and then killed by the army, was the one who stole it and he told Olga Behar what this meant.

The Communist Party was unenthusiastic, saying the sword was nothing but a museum apparatus. But as Fayad pointed out, the communist *guerrilla* had never shown interest in nationalism while the M-19, on the other hand, felt it had to capture national feeling and their thoughts turned towards the sword kept in the museum of the Liberator, the house where he had stayed at the foot of the mountain in what is now downtown.

"This was not simply to reappropriate the history of the Liberator," explained Fayad. "It was to recommence his struggle, to enlarge it, to go back to the nation which was constructed by his sword and invigorate it. It was to continue that history. That is why we took the sword."

Fayad felt something special. After securing the museum guards at gunpoint, he then had to break through the glass case.

"The silence is like a tomb in that colonial house. Ancient. Old. You can feel the silence. That moment was magical. It was great. The silence made it profound. I couldn't break through. I tried again. The glass tinkled as if it had broken into millions of fragments and fell to the floor. I put my hand into the urn and withdrew the sword and the spurs. I put them into one of those shoulderbags that the Indians make."

We acknowledge the magic — similar to that in the spirit queen's mountain except that Fayad is not out to save himself so much as remake an entire Nation-State. We note his principal means here is not force of arms but force of ritual — of transgression, the sacrilegious act become sacred in and of itself through stealing the sword of state for the overthrow of that state. Fayad is a revolutionary. The pilgrims to the enchanted mountain are not. But the magic they are stealing and making through that stealing is the same.

The ritual here is a defacement which allows sacred powers to emerge — in this case from the stupendously evocative wound of ambivalence which, in the secular aura of the modern state, is provided by the shrine posing as museum. Defacement is the holiest of acts because it not only draws out and exposes the magic within, but redoubles that magic and thus bears, in relation to the force of the Liberator, the unmistakable mark of the spirit queen herself. This is not only enchantment, but ecstasy.

This is enchantment not so much of the sacred history of the dead but of the shock of its shattering, the music of fragments. . . . And that is why this rupture is more than reappropriation of the past, of the sword from an urn become tomb become womb from which Fayad also extracts the Liberator's spurs, bringing forth together with this association with his magic steed the supreme macho embellishment of the fighting cock. The shattering has become no less important in these acts of sacrilege and despoliation than the impulse to re-gather the whole and make it complete once again. For the music of the fragments was there all along in the utopic revolutionary zeal and dashing purpose, the spurs gouging the flanks of the animal that is both the forwardness of history and the Nation-State in its white, rearing, majesty. Who rides this animal into the sunset of the school textbooks of history, locked arm in arm with the Chief Justice and Captain Mission? Who else but the Liberator whose spurs Fayad deftly deposits, along with the sword, into one of those shoulder bags that the Indians make.

Fayad's account of this ecstatic act of redemption is made even more iconic by the fact that close to if not actually overlooking the glass case with the sword in this very same museum hangs the 1819 portrait by José Pedro Figueroa of the Liberator with his arm firmly around an enigmatic and tiny woman, *la india*, Spanish-featured but adorned with the European symbols of America, pearls and fruits, bow and arrows. This doll-like woman, America herself, now freed from the colonial embrace, passes in her moment of Independence to the protective clasp of the Liberator.

This woman must be the spirit queen, the anticipation, we might say, of the spirit queen, awaiting her mountain.

And what is uncanny in Figuero's painting is not only how it anticipates her future coming by a century or a century and a half, but how it anticipates her intimate and magical connection with the Liberator, Fayad, for all his magnificent shattering, thus doing little more than reinstigating the eternal return involved in the violent making and breaking of stately being across the female form.

The sword of course is Hobbes' (s)word wherein word and force congeal in the purity of their extremes and in Fayad's hand it does more than symbolize the magical properties of the state apparatus and its relation to violence. The sword acquires the properties of a fetish, and does so through defacement.

What we have to appreciate here is not only the brilliant spontaneity of the ritual drama involved in Fayad's theft, but a specific yet largely unacknowledged art-form of sacrilege, which the Communist Party, working on more utilitarian and realist understandings of politics, could not visualize, calling the sword nothing but a "museum apparatus."

What we see here, as Claude Lévi-Strauss suggests for incest and bestiality, is sacrilege as an inversion of sacrifice — it being his understanding that sacrifice involves the mediation of extremes by some object that connects the extremes metonymically, not metaphorically, and has to be extinguished in the process.

This object is of course the sword wherein word and force congeal in the unity of their extremes.

In eliminating the object and hence contiguity between extremes, sacrifice provides an empty space which communion with the deity now fills as a sort of compensatory contiguity.

What distinguishes yet also connects sacrifice and sacrilege is how we visualize this charged emptiness, the mark of the sacred. For if with sacrifice it is the emptiness that fulfills, with sacrilege it is the filling of the space with the extremes that not so much fulfills as spills over in proliferating cascades. . . .

And in stealing the sword, as with spirit possession, an enormous burden is placed on the theater of metonymy, on literalizing metaphor by having the sword perform its swordness combining, in their extremity, force and word — a task made electrifyingly easy by the fact that it is precisely the function of the sword of state to mediate between force and word. As Hobbes reminds us, "Covenants without the sword are but words."

Yet when Fayad first grasped it he was surprised how small it was.

Nevertheless, "What a feeling to possess it, to grasp it!"

"What I hold in my hand is not an old weapon but the true history of our country, a history that we are going to remake. . . . In grasping this sword one feels him, one feels the presence of the Liberator. And one feels an immense compromise."

"Sacrifice destroys that which it consecrates," says Bataille, in which case sacrilege is not simply the inversion of sacrifice so much as sacrifice redoubled, involving the sacrifice of sacrifice, the loss of loss.

Fayad was sacrificed too. Tortured. Released. Then killed in a prolonged shootout with the army. It was a sequence of sacrifices, of violence, of losses, of unproductive expenditures. All *guerrilla* war invites these acts of stately expenditure. The more blood the better.

Moreover the sword was not merely stolen through an act of sacrilege, but was lost, as we shall see, to history itself. That is one form of loss. Disappearance. Disappearance of the object itself.

But how much more demanding is the loss necessitated by both sacrifice and sacrilege when these very rituals are transformed into the comic-absurd of state terror?

As fetish the care lavished on this stolen sword was more than it ever received from the state.

A *compañero* fell into the hands of the police. He did not know exactly where they had hidden the sword but he did know in what part of the city it was. Fayad and his friends knew the authorities would torture him and might well invade and ransack every single house in that zone to get the sword back. So they had to move it.

"It was put into a box, with vaseline, with all the protection given by grease, and after that a layer of plastic and then of pitch. It got bigger and bigger until we had to place it in a huge wooden box. It looked like a coffin. It wouldn't fit in the trunk of the car and we had to let half of it stick out."

They tied a red flag to the end of the protrusion.

Something added. It got bigger and bigger. When will it stop growing this mighty fetish-power in grease and plastic, now in a coffin protruding from a car winding through the ghoulish streets of the capital to escape the police?

They decided to take a photo of themselves together with the sword figuring that if the police knew who they were, they had nothing to lose and everything to gain coming out this way. Once again they had to risk their lives crossing the city, this time to find a camera, only to discover that none of them knew how to use it. They tried anyway, each one posing with the sword. But the photos were of such poor quality as to be unpublishable.

When Vera Grabe, also of the M-19 *guerrilla*, was interviewed by Olga Behar, she described how as she was being tortured by the army one of their persistent questions was the whereabouts of the sword. She could hear Fayad screaming in an adjacent cell. And his resistance, she said, gave her strength to hang on and pull through.

The first demands sacrifice, says Water Benjamin, distinguishing mythic from divine violence. The second accepts it. The first preserves law. The second destroys it. Here mythic violence dramatically confronts the sacrilege committed by divine violence for it must be recognized that during its first few years of operation the M-19 stood out not only for its commitment to political theater — such as the stealing of the sword — but for a commitment, at times explicit, at times oblique, to a populist politics that was profoundly ambivalent about taking state power instead of destroying that power.

In the end, but there is no end, the divine violence authorizing revolutionary struggle on the part of the M-19 lost out to the mythic force of the state making law as the M-19 surrendered their arms and entered parliament to suffer humiliating defeats at the polls. Fayad's screams as much as Vera Grabe's live on to haunt this laying down of arms and divine violence returns to the incubator of popular revolt and barely suppressed dreams of the apocalypse. But we, who register the violence inflicted on the bodies of the M-19 by the police apparatus no less than we must register the violence of the *guerrilla*, can never make the mistake of equating these two violences even as we are forced to try to understand their necessary and terrible intertwinement.

As for the Liberator's stolen sword, real life picks up where the screams haunt us and does so in the living theater of kitsch, testimony to the blending of absurdity with mythic violence in the formation of state terror.

In March 1990 it was reported in the daily papers that Jaime Bateman, legendary leader of the M-19 (who died mysteriously in a flight to Panama over the Darien Gap), had entrusted the sword to Fidel Castro on condition it be returned when the M-19 took the revolution to power. But because they had neither assumed power nor revolution, Fidel Castro refused. Hence, the M-19 was taking the case of the stolen sword to the Organization of American States to see justice done, while the sword rests with Fidel . . . until the revolution.

But we know that the Liberator had many swords, perhaps more than we can count, and the difference between the mythic violence of the state and the divine violence of destruction of law rests finally on the illusion of sword for swords that her presence as queen, sovereign of the soulful world, allows to the world of swordful states. For the Liberator grasps not only his sword, but also his spirit queen that is America, abject, but aloof, marking the entrance through the earth to the sublime powers of magical defacement that promise freedom.

This would return us to the view of the modern state as the privileged staging-ground of the really made up bound to thickness, density, screens, endless scenarios involving the staging of hidden innerness. That it is the fate of woman to mark this and its magic is perhaps well known but always shocking — for what cannot be articulated, by definition, and this is the only depth worth talking about, is the horror of the mute-absurd of the violence upon which all states are not only founded but founder in their attempts to extract holiness from the space of death and the imagination of the child.

18 — *Pilgrimage as Method*

Pilgrimage is what the people do who go to the mountain and is analogous to translation —between home and shrine, between pro-fane and sacred, and, not least, between official and unofficial voices. Pilgrimage pro-vides a model of explanation-as-translation that we might find congenial too, not one claiming universal objectivity clinging to the metaphors of causation transcendent over the concrete particular, but instead a mode of activating activity which does not erase the image or the event or the object but maintains the ghost of the translated within the translation, allowing us to witness the presence within the other, the imprint and the play between — as between official and unofficial voices, as between a school his-tory textbook and magical gateways on a mountain, as between a totalized "people" and its image reflected in the (magic) mirror of historical construction of the Subject. To be a pilgrim is to travel tic-wise across this nervy wasteland of facial impulses, await-ing the illumination that occurs with the inter-ruption to the circuit—a sort of gift, where image and body seize.

A shrine that facilitates spirit possession is like this too — an "explanation" of the sort I am offering even as it escapes me in changing the world, a circle of exchange interrupted by the gift in the form of the shrine that is here called the gateway because it leads beyond the circle, just as the gift in epitomizing the circle of society necessarily ruptures the circuit of exchange. It cannot be contained in the equations of obligation — to give, to receive, and to pay back. Many explanations do stay within the circle of exchange; this is ritual in the sense of mindless and obsessional repetition. Others not only permit the rupture but are just that, testimony to unproductive expenditure, the need to squander.

So what of the imagined world unreeling before your eyes right now by means of my talk and pictures? For are not we, in the safe-house of our reading, watching them watching and becoming possessed, transformed by other worlds, into other worlds, first them . . . then us? Is not this — our presence, our elbowing our way in, our witness, our being shown — the strangest thing of all in this entire strangeness, or, if not that, at least the ingredient most crucial for strangeness to occur, and hence, what amounts to the same thing but in another idiom, are we not rendering the metaphoric carnal and the imagination material, are we not here and now in our very and busy-bodiedness an arc in the vast circuit of exchange for different intensities transmuting substance and sign through an act of transposition (with all its assembling, divisions, and intermittence)? And is this not the form of this transposing text held in your hands . . . "the talmudic melody questions . . . and a great screw, proud in its entirety, humble in its turns, twists from small, distant beginnings in the direction of the one who questions."

In the direction of the one who questions. This brings us back to pilgrimage as method circling between sacred and profane, not so much explaining as absorbing the slow-release shock, figuring the figures in other rites oscillating in the blurred but bright light of transgression yoked to the Law of the Father undershot with the presence of the body of the mother, brooding, immense, bejeweled with sparkling shrines, gateways to her secrets shrouded with cloud rising from the plain.

For the task of much of cultural anthropology, no less than of certain branches of historiography, has been, and will increasingly continue to be, the storing in modernity of what are taken to be pre-modern practises such as spirit possession and magic, thereby contributing,

for good or for bad, to the reservoir of authoritative, estranging, literal-
ities on which so much of our contemporary language is based in its
conjuring of the back-then and the over-there for contemporary purpose if not profane illumination.

☐ —— BIBLIOGRAPHY

Books and Articles that Helped the Writing of this Book

Abrams, Philip. "Notes on the Difficulty of Studying the State." *The Journal of Historical Sociology* 1, no.1 (1988): 58–89.

Anderson, Bennedict. *Imagined Communities*. New York: Verso, 1983.

Asturias, Miguel Angel. *El señor presidente*. Trans. Frances Partridge. New York: Atheneum, 1982.

Barreto, Daisy, J. *María Lionza: mito e historia*. Caracas: Universidad Central de Venezuela, 1987.

———. "Perspectiva histórica del mito y culto a María Lionza." *Boletín Américanista* 39–40 (1990): 9–26.

Bataille, Georges. *The Accursed Share: An Essay On General Economy*, 3 vols. Trans. Robert Hurley. New York: Zone Books, 1988.

———. "The Notion of Expenditure." In *Visions of Excess. Selected Writings, 1927–1939*, ed. Allan Stoekel, 116–29. Minnesota: University of Minnesota Press, 1985.

———. "The Obelisk." In *Visions of Excess. Selected Writings, 1927–1939*, ed. Allan Stoekel, 213–22. Minnesota: University of Minnesota Press, 1985.

Becket, Samuel. *Proust*. New York: Grove, 1970.

Behar, Olga. *Las guerras de la paz*. Bogotá: Planeta, 1985.

Benjamin, Walter. "Critique of Violence." In *Reflections*, ed. Peter Demetz, Trans. Edmund Jephcott, 277–301. New York: Harcourt Brace Jovanovich, 1978.

Benjamin, Walter. "The Storyteller: Reflections on the Work of Nikolai Leskov." In *Illuminations*, ed. Hannah Arendt, trans. Harry Zohn, 83–110. New York: Schocken, 1969.

Boulton, Alfredo. *Historia de la pintura en Venezuela*, 2 vols. Caracas: Editorial Arte, 1968.

Boddy, Janice. "Spirit Possession Revisited: Beyond Instrumentality." *Annual Review of Anthropology* 24 (1994): 407–34.

Bravo Díaz, María Josefina. *Mi historia de Venezuela: educación basica*. Caracas: Colegial Bolivariana, 1986.

Briceño, Jacqueline de Clarac. "El culto de María Lionza." *América Indigena* 30, no.2 (April, 1970): 359–74.

———. "Una religión en formación en una sociedad petrolera." *Boletín Antropológico*, Centro de Investigaciones del Museo Arqueológico, Merida, 4 (November–December, 1983): 28–35.

Brown, Norman O. *Love's Body*. Berkeley and Los Angeles: University of California Press, 1966.

Brown, Peter. *The Cult of the Saints: Its Rise and Function in Latin Christianity*. Chicago: University of Chicago Press, 1981.

Burroughs, William S. *Cities of the Red Night*. New York: Holt, Rhinehart, and Winston, 1981.

Cabrera, Lydia. *El monte, igbo, ewe, orisha nititi nfinda (notas sobre las religiones, la magia, las supersticiones y el folklore de los negros criollos y del pueblo de Cuba)*. Miami, FL: Ediciones C. R., 1971.

Caillois, Roger. "The Sociology of the Executioner." In *The College of Sociology: 1937–39*, ed. Denis Hollier, trans. Betsy Wing, 233–47. Minneapolis: University of Minnesota Press, 1988.

Camacho, Simón. "Recuerdos de Santa Marta, 1842." In *Memorias de Carmelo Fernández*, 109–142. Biblioteca de la Academia Nacional de Historia. 7. Caracas: Fuentes Para La Historia Republicana de Venezuela, 1973.

Canetti, Elias. *Crowds and Power*. New York: Farrar Straus Giroux, 1984.

Carpentier, Alejo. *El recurso del metodo: una novela*. Mexico, D.F.: Siglo Veintiuno, 1977.

Carrera Damas, German. *El culto a Bolívar*. Caracas: Universidad Central de Venezuela, 1973.

———. *Venezuela: proyecto nacional y poder social*. Barcelona: Editorial Critica, 1986.

Clastres, Pierre. *Society Against the State*. trans. Robert Hurley. New York: Zone, 1989.

Conrad, Joseph. *Nostromo: A Tale of the Seaboard*. London: Dent, 1960.

Deleuze, Giles and Félix Guattari. *A Thousand Plateaus: Capitalism and Schizophrenia*. Trans. Brian Massumi. Minneapolis: University of Minnesota Press, 1987.

Documents: Doctrines, Archéologie, Beaux-Arts, Ethnographie, Varietiés. Années 1929 et 1930, 2 vols. Paris: Editions Jean-Michel Place, 1991.

Dumezil, Georges. *The Destiny of a King*. University of Chicago Press: Chicago and London, 1973.

Elsaesser, Thomas. "Dada/Cinema?" *Dada and Surrealist Film*. Edited by Rudolf E. Kuenzli, pp. 13–27. New York: Willis Locker and Owens, 1987.

Ernst, Adofo. *La exposión nacional de Venezuela en 1883: Obra escrita de orden del Ilustre Americano, General Guzmán Blanco*. Caracas: Ministerio de Fomento, 1884.

Ewell, Judith. *Venezuela: A Century of Change*. Stanford: Stanford University Press, 1984.

Fleming, E. McClung. "The American Image as Indian Princess: 1765–1783." *The Winterthur Portfolio* 2 (1965): 65–81.

Freud, Sigmund. *Totem and Taboo*. In *The Standard Edition of the Complete Psychological Works of Sigmund Freud*, ed. and trans. James Stratchey, vol 13. London: The Hogarth Press, 1958.

García Gavidia, Nelly. *Posesión y ambivalencia en el culto a María Lionza: notas para una tipología de los cultos de posesión existentes en la América del Sur*. Maracaibo: Facultad Experimental de Ciencias, Universidad de Zulua, 1987.

García Marquez, Gabriel. *El general en su laberinto*. Bogotá: Oveja Negra,1989.

———. *The Autumn of the Patriarch*. Trans. Gregory Rabassa. New York: Avon, 1976.

George, Susan and F. Sabelli. *Faith and Credit*. New York: Harper Collins, 1994.

Gilchrist, Lucia. *La India Catalina*. Bogotá: Tercer Mundo, 1979.

Hegel, G.W. F. *Elements of the Philosophy of Right*. Ed. Allen Wood, trans. H. B. Nisbet. Cambridge: Cambridge University Press. 1991.

———. *The Philosophy of History*. trans. J. Baillie. New York: Dover, 1956.

———. *The Phenomenology of Mind*. trans. J. B. Baillie.New York: Harper and Row, 1967.

Herrea Luque, Francisco. Bolívar de carne y hueso y otros ensayos. Caracas: Pomaire, 1987.

Hertz, Neil. "Medusa's Head: Male Hysteria under Political Pressure," In *The End of the Line: Essays on Psychoanalysis and the Sublime*. New York: Columbia University Press, 1985.

Hobbes, Thomas. *Leviathan*. New York and London: Collier, 1962.

Horkheimer, Max and Theodore W., Adorno. *The Dialectic of Enlightenment*. Trans. John Cummming. New York: Continuum, 1987.

Kantorowicz, Ernst H. *The King's Two Bodies: A Study in Mediaeval Political Theology*. Princeton, N.J.: Princeton University Press,1957.

Kojeve, Alexandre. *Introduction to the Reading of Hegel: Lectures on the Phenomenonology of Spririt*. Ed. by Alan Bloom. Ithaca and London: Cornell University Press, 1969.

Kristeva, Julia. *Powers of Horror: An Essay on Abjection*. Trans. Leon S. Roudiez. New York: Columbia University Press, 1982.

Lefort, Claude. *The Political Forms of Modern Society: Bureaucracy, Democracy, Totalitarianism*. Cambrdge, Mass.: Mit Press, 1986.

Leiris, Michel. *Manhood: A Journey from Childhood to the Fierce Order of Virility*. Translated by Richard Howard. San Francisco: North Point Press, 1984.

————. "The Sacred in Everyday Life." In *The College of Sociology; 1937–39*, ed. by Denis Hollier, 98–102. Minneapolis: University of Minnesota Press, 1986.

————. *La Possession et ses aspects théâtraux chez les Éthiopiens de Gondar*. Paris: Plon, 1958.

Lenin, Vladmir Illych. *The State and Revolution*. Foreign Languages Press: Peking, 1965.

Levi-Strauss, Claude. *The Savage Mind*. Chicago: University of Chicago Press, 1966.

Levine, Daniel H. *The Catholic Church in Venezuela and Colombia*. Princeton, N.J.: Princeton University Press, 1981.

Lewis, Mark. "What is to be Done?" Art and Politics after the Fall . . ." *Ideology and Power in the Age of Lenin in Ruins*. Ed. Arthur and Marylouise Kroker, 1–20. New York: St. Martin's Press, 1991.

Luque, Francisco Herrera. *Boves: el urogallo*. Caracas:Pomaire, 1987.

Margolies, Luise. "José Gregorio Hernández: The Historical Development of a Venezuelan Popular Saint." *Studies in Latin American Popular Culture* 3 (1984): 28–46.

Martin, Gustavo. *Magia y religión en la Venezuela contemporánea*. Caracas:Universidad Central de Venezuela, 1983.

Marx, Karl. *Capital: A Critique of Political Economy*, 3 vols. New York: International Publishers. 1967.

————. *Grundrisse: Foundations of the Critique of Political Economy. (Rough Draft).* Trans. Martin Nicolaus. Harmondsworth: Penguin Books, 1973.

Melville, Herman. *Benito Cereno.* London: Nonesuch Press, 1926.

Museo de Arte Contemporáneo de Caracas. *Pedro Centeno Vallenilla.* Caracas: Museo de Arte Contemporáneo, 1991.

Nairn, Tom. *The Enchanted Glass: Britain and Its Monarchy.* London: Hutchinson Radius, 1988.

Nietzsche, Friedrich. *The Gay Science.* Trans. Walter Kaufmann. New York: Vintage, 1974.

Ortner, Sherry. "The Virgin and the State." *Feminist Studies* 4, no.3 (1978): 19–36.

Palenzuela, Juan Carlos. *Primeros monumentos en Venezuela a Simón Bolívar.* Caracas: Biblioteca de la Academia Nacional de la Historia, 1983.

Pividal, Francisco. *Bolívar: pensamiento precursor del antimperialismo.* Caracas: Ateneo de Caracas, 1983.

Plato. *The Republic.* Trans. Desmond Lee. Harmondsworth, Middlesex: Penguin, 1974.

Pollak-Eltz, Angelina. *María Lionza: mito y culto venezolano.* (Segunda edición revisada y ampliada.) Caracas: Universidad Catolica Andres Bello, 1985.

Puentes, Milton. *Bolívar, padre de las izquierdas Liberales.* Bogotá: Tipografia Hispana, n.d.

Rivero, Armando. *María Lionza: La diosa del amor y de la fortuna. Mito y leyendas hechos realidad desde hace más de 200 años.* Caracas: David Rivero, n.d.

Rouget, Gilbert. *Music and Trance: A Theory of the Relations Between Music and Possession.* Trans. B. Biebuyck. Chicago: University of Chicago Press, 1980.

Salas de Lecuna, Yolanda. *Bolívar y la historia en la conciencia popular.* (With the collaboration of Norma González Viloria and Ronny Velásquez), Caracas: Universidad Símon Bolívar; Instituto de Altos Estudios de América Latina, 1987.

Schmidt, Carl. *Political Theology.* Trans. George Schwab. Cambridge, Mass.: MIT Press, 1988.

Schivelbusch, Wolfgang. *The Railway Journey: The Industrialization of Time and Space in the 19th Century.* Berkeley: University of California Press, 1977.

Shell, Marc. *Money, Language, and Thought: Literary and Philosophic*

Economies from the Medieval to the Modern Era. Baltimore, Md.: Johns Hopkins University Press, 1993.

Sociedad Bolivariana de Venezuela. *Estatuto general.* Caracas:Centro Bolivariano de San Carlos, Estado Cojedes, 1975.

Sociedad Bolivariano de Venezuela; Centro de Estado Zulia. *Cronología del Libertador.* Eitorial Maracaibo, 1980.

Tsing, Anna. *In The Realm of the Diamond Queen.* Princeton: Princeton University Press, 1994.

Toro, Fermin. "Descripción de las honras funebres consagradas a los restos del Libertador Simón Bolívar." In *Reflexiones sobre la ley de 10 de abril de 1834 y otras obras*, 203–53. Caracas: Ministerio de Educacion Nacional, 1941.

Turner, Victor and Edith Turner. *Image and Pilgrimage in Christian Culture: Anthropological Perspectives.* New York: Columbia University Press, 1978.

Valencia, Guillermo. *La glorificación del Libertador.* Bogotá: Banco de la Republica, 1980

Vargas, Teniente Francisco Alejandro. *Guaicaipuro: El cacique de los Teques.* Caracas, 1946.

Wilgus, A. Curtis. *South American Dictators: During The First Century of Independence.* New York: Russell and Russell, 1937.

Wills Pradilla, Jorgé (ed.). *La agonía, la muerte y los funerales del libertador en 1830 y la exhumación de sus restos en 1842; la última enfermedad, los últimos momentos y los funerales de Simón Bolívar, Libertador de Colombia y del Peru por su médico de cabecera el Dr. A. P. Révérend.* Bogotá: Minerva, 1930.

Wilson, Stephen. Ed. *Saints and Their Cults: Studies in Religious Sociology, Folklore and History.* Cambridge: Cambridge University Press, 1983.